» The Book of Hours

D1194358

» Rainer Maria Rilke

The Book *of* Hours

Prayers to a Lowly God

A BILINGUAL EDITION

TRANSLATED FROM THE GERMAN AND

WITH AN INTRODUCTION AND NOTES

BY ANNEMARIE S. KIDDER

NORTHWESTERN UNIVERSITY PRESS

EVANSTON, ILLINOIS

Northwestern University Press
www.nupress.northwestern.edu

Printed in the United States of America

10 9 8 7 6 5 4

ISBN-13: 978-0-8101-1888-1
ISBN-10: 0-8101-1888-2

Library of Congress Cataloging-in-Publication Data

Rilke, Rainer Maria, 1875–1926.
  [Stundenbuch. English & German]
  The book of hours : prayers to a lowly god / Rainer Maria Rilke ;
translated from the German and with an introduction and notes by
Annemarie S. Kidder.— A bilingual ed.
      p. cm.
Includes bibliographical references.
  ISBN 0-8101-1888-2 (alk. paper)
  I. Kidder, Annemarie S. II. Title.
  PT2635.I65 S72513 2001
  831'.912—dc21

                                        2001004162

∞ The paper used in this publication meets the minimum
requirements of the American National Standard for Information
Sciences—Permanence of Paper for Printed Library Materials,
ANSI Z39.48-1992.

» Contents

» Acknowledgments

The translation of this book is the result of the efforts of many people, some who have pointed me toward Rilke's poetry and others who have lent me the energy to complete the work. In particular, I want to thank the deaconesses of the Motherhouse Tabea in Hamburg, Germany, for introducing me to *The Book of Hours* while I lived and worked with them during the summer of 1987. Their life of celibacy, poverty, and service appeared to have its counterpart in Rilke's praying monk and prompted me to begin writing prayers in poetic form in my native German tongue. Later, during my theological studies at Southern Seminary in Louisville, Kentucky, these prayers were translated into English, with more English poetry following over the years. The idea to translate the book came in 1997 when a colleague quoted to me an English excerpt from *The Book of Hours* and when, subsequently, a friend casually mentioned how much she enjoyed Rilke's *Book of Hours*. My gratitude goes to two masters of German poetic translation into English, Walter Arndt and Walter Kaufmann, whose work has given me continued guidance and inspiration and the courage to look beyond the literal translation of the word. Also, I thank the members and staff of First Presbyterian Church, Battle Creek, for their support in reading and listening to portions of the translated manuscript. Most of all, I want to thank my mother, Berta Schuh, and my grandmother, Berta Glaser, who both died before I could share Rilke with them, for instilling in me an early love for poetry and for never tiring of reading my poetic compositions and showing me theirs in turn.

Annemarie S. Kidder
Cincinnati, Ohio
Easter 2001

» Translator's Introduction

Rainer Maria Rilke (1875–1926) always insisted that *The Book of Hours* should not be thought of as a series of separate poems but as one long poem. That was the way he wrote it, and he emphasized the importance of the book's being published with a uniform typographical appearance. There were to be no emphatic breaks, except for those between the three books. This introduction follows this principle and instead of commenting on particular passages or poems examines each book and its prominent themes as a whole. For additional information, the reader is referred to the notes at the end of the book and a number of secondary works. All translations of poems, diary entries, and letter excerpts are mine.

"THE BOOK OF THE MONKISH LIFE"

The Book of Hours was first published at Christmas of 1905. It consists of three parts of which the first part, "The Book of the Monkish Life," was written in its first draft between September 20 and October 14, 1899. The poems represent the conversations of a Russian monk-painter with God, and Rilke had originally called it *The Prayers.* He chose the final title based on the French medieval tradition of *livres d'heures,* which were devotional prayer books for lay use. It is filled with impressions from Italy and Russia.

From April 15 until the end of June 1898, Rilke had stayed in Florence, where he made the acquaintance of the Italian masters of painting and sculpture, notably of the Renaissance. His "Florentine Diary," contained in *Tagebücher aus der Frühzeit,* edited by his daughter Ruth and her husband and published in 1942 by Insel Verlag, is filled with impressions of his visits to churches, museums, palazzi, and cemeteries. Many of the motifs found in "The

Book of the Monkish Life" are recorded in sketches here. Rilke grapples with the role of the painter in society and the painter's motivation as artist. Does the painter serve the public primarily in bringing them joy, "furthering their digestion and [their] decorating their living room with the obliging piece of art"? Or is painting, and art in general, as Rilke maintains, "a path to freedom," where the artist tears the chains apart "not with an ugly and wild violence" but by "growing out of them" gradually (32–33)?

For Rilke, the duty of the artist is to travel the austere journey of self-discovery. He compares this journey to life in a religious order, whereby the artist practices releasing all trifling and temporary things as by placing them outside the door, purging his or her self of them, in order to be left with the wide-open space of a festive interior home, or castle (34). It is ultimately a journey that will lead to the sacrifice, the will to solitude.

In Italy, Rilke wonders about the relationship between the artist and the church—art's benefactor. He maintains that the artist did not create to please a commissioning church, to instill culture in an uncivilized people, to instruct a spiritually devoid populace; instead, the artist sought to still his or her own longing for self-discovery. All these painters, Rilke says, even "if some of them wore monk's habits and painted on praying knees . . . had only one faith and one religious conviction burned in them: the longing search [*Sehnsucht*] for themselves" (37).

The indirect and unwitting role of the organized church, then, which Rilke interchangeably calls religion, is to provide an outlet for all those who are not artists. For "religion is the art of the nonartistic. They become productive in prayer: they formulate their love and gratitude and their longing and free themselves in this way" (38). Thus the nonartistic need religion, be it only one based on a common historic agreement. For "being an atheist means in that sense being a barbarian" (38).

But there is danger in allowing the church or religious practice to quench one's continued longing and quest for self-discovery. Those especially, Rilke says, who have the deepest longing do not know exactly for what. And so they are easily sidetracked when "told by the tempter: 'It's God and His mercy you are longing for; renounce yourselves, and you will find Him'; whereupon they renounce themselves and lose their longing" altogether (42).

People, artists, who maintain this longing do not need to erect or decorate churches. For they themselves become churches who can offer themselves up to God as holy temples. "Nothing personal is to remain," Rilke says. "We empty ourselves, we surrender, we unfold—until one day our gestures are found in swaying treetops and our smile is resurrected among the children who play underneath these trees" (68).

For Rilke, each person is like a church, covered by festive frescoes. In childhood, when the riches are yet accessible, it is too dark inside to see them. And then, as it gets lighter, the foolhardiness of adolescence arrives and with that the wrong kind of longings and the thirsting desires, which manage to cover the riches up from wall to wall. Some advance in years without ever suspecting the old riches underneath the plain poverty. But those will be blessed who eventually feel them, find them, and quietly unearth them (101).

Toward the end of the "Florentine Diary," Rilke emerges not as the self-seeking artist but as one who sees the need to share his findings so as to help others free themselves from the dark fetters within. In conversations with other boarders at his hotel, including a Russian woman, he discovers an inner force able to comfort and lend hope to others. "I feel," he says, "as if I had to convert all those who hesitate and doubt; for I have more power within than I can manage to hold in words, and want to use it to free people from their strange fear, the same fear I escaped from" (98).

The role of the artist, then, is to free people from their fears, to prepare the way for the birth of "some force" (119). This "force" will arrive at long last and "will carry everything in Himself that had its effect on us and drives us; for He will be the largest space, full of every power imaginable. Only One will reach this state, while all others are the forebears of this Lonely One. Nothing will exist apart from Him; for trees and mountains, clouds and waves were only symbols of His reality" (119) and "each generation becomes like a chain leading from God to God." Rilke sums up the essence of "The Book of the Monkish Life" by saying that we "are the forebears of a God who are reaching ahead into the centuries by our deepest moments of loneliness until He can have His beginning" (120).

The other country Rilke was deeply impressed with, probably more so than any other during his writing of "The Book of the Monkish Life," was Russia. Unlike with Italy, we have no notebook or diary of Rilke's to draw from. Commentary consists of letters written to friends, an essay titled "Russian Art," and the original manuscript of the first draft of "The Book of the Monkish Life" placed in the hands of his traveling companion, onetime lover, and lifelong friend Lou Andreas-Salomé, for whose benefit he wrote the "Florentine Diary" and the two subsequent ones contained in *Tagebücher aus der Frühzeit*.

Rilke, Lou, and Lou's husband, Carl Andreas, left for Moscow in April 25, 1899. They returned from Petersburg via Danzig to Schmargendorf on June 18. One finds great differences between the first draft of the manuscript given to Lou and the published version of "The Book of the Monkish Life," which is based on two later manuscripts, known as B and C. This first draft, called Manuscript A, was not accessible to the general public until 1963, when it appeared in the third volume of Rilke's *Sämtliche Werke*. It had been published previously as part of Ruth Mövius's dissertation titled *Rainer Maria Rilkes Stunden-Buch: Entstehung und Gehalt* in 1937 by Insel Verlag. Manuscript A contains many prose inserts that interpret the poems, and it includes additional poems. Included also is a letter from the Russian monk turned painter, Apostol, who is the protagonist of "The Book of the Monkish Life," to the Metropolitan, the highest-ranking church official of the Eastern church. This painter-monk expresses Rilke's observations on the art seen in Russia, notably iconography, in comparison with the paintings of the Italian Renaissance seen on his 1898 trip to Italy. The monk consequently becomes the mouthpiece of Rilke's view of the difference between Western and Eastern art. Mövius says, "Rilke immerses himself totally into this monk, so that eventually he becomes him" (52).

The monk is painting in prescribed Eastern style, but he has read about other styles of painting quite different from his, which leaves him confused, anxious, and concerned. According to the monk, the West has placed God in a finite and human framework of time and space, of form and function. He believes that this is sinful, irreverent, and dangerous. While the monk's main initial interest is painting, later on it leads to more general reflections on art, including speculations about God. The monk writes to the Metropolitan:

> *Honorable Father, so much wiser in years,*
> *punish me, if I should speak vanity.*
> *They have squandered God while we are*
> *frugal with our God and place*
> *each deed of His and all that pleased us*
> *in some cooling box; we smooth*
> *each present tense just like a dress*
> *and hide our loot amidst the sense*
> *that everything is God which runs*
> *unnamed through our hands.*
>
> (*Sämtliche Werke,* 3:363)

The result of Western art's rushed, impatient strokes and its squandering God is that God ultimately runs away and hides, as the monk points out in his letter to the Metropolitan:

> *God runs away from everything depicted*
> *that sought to find His coloring over time;*
> *in any painting only His cloak remains*
> *where by hurried ones He had been enshrined;*
> *God has withdrawn into His farthest worlds*
> *and the painter's hand, abandoned, errs.*
>
> (3:363)

The Renaissance works of art, then, are empty shells, removed from people's experience, and cannot help one find God. The icon, on the other hand, is a receptacle the people fill with their experience and which, in turn, allows them to envision and experience God. In Rilke's essay "Russische Kunst," contained in the fifth volume of his *Sämtliche Werke,* he describes the Russian people as those "whose entirety of experience is of a religious nature and so strong that they unveil a beauty [of God] to us in their darkened Byzantine pictures that the mechanical-type copies of the Greek monks of Athos never had." In fact, the Russian people are able to "espy countless madonnas in the hollow icons and their creative longing constantly enlivens the empty ovals turning them into mild faces" (5:495–96).

The monk fears that unless the Russian style of religious painting is maintained, remaining "untainted" by the so-called Latin heresy of Western ideas, God might withdraw from people altogether.

> *He came, chased after in the world,*
> *and they have all blinded Him:*
> *some depicted Him as poor,*

others displayed Him in lavish riches—
and no nation was silent about Him.
Away from stone and brows He climbed,
disappointed by the clamor, into the night.
"Do you have a dress?" He had asked us.
And we are almost the last ones who do.
What if we chase Him away too . . . ?

(3:366)

The emphasis of the monk's letter to the Metropolitan is to insist upon keeping God from withdrawing by adhering to the artistic principles of Orthodox tradition. The letter stresses the human effort and faithfulness necessary to allow for God's visibility, manifestation, and ultimately God's well-being. God is viewed by Rilke as almost helplessly dependent on the artist, who functions as translator and whose medium, painting, allows the masses to experience God. This assertion is not meant as arrogance, irreverence, or even blasphemy. Instead, it is based on the monk's, and Rilke's, conviction that both God and the person are interconnected and benefit and grow by their dynamic relationship with each other. In a letter of January 1900, Rilke writes about the Russian people in whom "that element might be realized which I only dare suggest in uncertain words: that their God (who is not yet completed) and their art (which is not yet completed) are steadily unfolding side by side in mutual influence" (*Rainer Maria Rilke*, 96).

But not only painting becomes this medium by which the artist can allow God to become manifest; poetry and song do as well. "The Book of the Monkish Life" concludes by comparing God to a blind singer, a *kobzar*, who has lost his songs. Rilke had commented on these singers in a short story titled "Das Lied von der Gerechtigkeit" ("The Song of Justice") in his *Geschichten vom lieben Gott* (*Stories of God*), written less than a month after "The

Book of the Monkish Life." In the story, a tall black figure appears in the door, which was "one of the blind *kobzars,* an old man, who walked through the villages with his twelve-stringed bandura in hand" (*Sämtliche Werke,* 4:334), singing "The Song of Justice" and of whom Ewald, who hears the story, says, "This old man was God" (4:337). Rilke comments in his first draft of "The Book of the Monkish Life" on these singers, "of whom the monk had read in old chronicles . . . and who in days past had wandered through the huts in the vast Ukraine as evening came" (3:373). Now the monk wants to retrieve these songs, their melody and lyrics, and return them to their rightful owner. As a result, God is no longer just a blind old man, but God becomes God again.

"THE BOOK OF PILGRIMAGE"

Rilke wrote the second book contained in *The Book of Hours,* "The Book of Pilgrimage," during the week of September 18 to 25, 1901, in Westerwede, Germany. Again Russian imagery plays a role, but the focus is less on the specific art form of the icon and more on the various sites of Russia and especially the Ukraine. The title of the book refers to Rilke's second visit of Russia in the summer of 1900, which he considered a pilgrimage to his new homeland of choice. Only he and Lou Andreas-Salomé made the trip this time. Whereas the imagery of "The Book of the Monkish Life" is informed by Rilke's visit to the art galleries of Moscow and St. Petersburg, "The Book of Pilgrimage" draws on the Ukraine, especially Kiev and its Pechersk monastery.

On May 31, 1900, Rilke left for the Ukraine and returned from Petersburg for Berlin on August 22. Little is known from Rilke directly about his second Russia visit, especially in the Ukraine. There are brief references in his "Schmargendorf Diary," contained in *Tagebücher aus der Frühzeit,* some letters to his mother concerning Kiev, and Lou Andreas-Salomé's semiautobiographical novel *Rodinka* (1922). In a letter to his mother, Rilke writes about the Pechersk monastery with its ancient catacombs: "This is the holiest monastery in the entire kingdom. I have, lit candle in hand, walked about all these caves, once alone and another time with the other praying people . . . and I have determined that, before I leave Kiev, I will again . . . visit the catacombs" there (*Rainer Maria Rilke,* 102).

This monastery, also known as the Kievan Lavra, plays a prominent role in "The Book of Pilgrimage," where Rilke makes it the recurring locus of the monk's observations. As such, Rilke weaves his impressions of the monastery into the monk's reflections, observations, and prayers at five separate places in "The Book of Pilgrimage": first, in passing mention; second, in a rather detailed description of its underground cells and mummified monks buried there; third, when a large group of pilgrims gathers by one of the monastic wells; fourth, when a sick monk coming from the infirmary has a seizure; and finally at the end of the book as the monk is digging for God in the ground as one would for a treasure. Both accounts, of the throng of pilgrims gathering at the well and of the sick monk's seizures, are based on actual occurrences, which Lou Andreas-Salomé describes in some detail in *Rodinka*.

Kiev's monastery was a curiosity and a popular pilgrimage destination. Because it sat on the high bank of the Dnieper River, the founding monks had in the middle of the eleventh century been able to dig into the bank, establishing underground cells. At the time of Rilke's visit, the complex consisted of twenty-two churches (sixteen above ground, six underground), several monasteries, buildings for a printing press and administration, and the cave monastery. Only a century and a half earlier, the complex had counted seven small and three large cities,

120 villages, farms, and hamlets with a total population of 56,000, in addition to various monasteries lying outside its walls with a total population of 20,000. Rilke's visit explains his frequent use of images describing monastic communities and clusters of churches.

Other images are drawn from Rilke's trip up the Volga from Saratov to Jaroslavl, first by ship, later by boat. In a letter from Petersburg, July 31, 1900, he writes:

> To be on the Volga, this quietly rolling sea, for days and nights, many days and many nights: a wide, wide stream; high, high forest to the one bank, on the other deep heath, where even large cities sit in between like huts and tents.—One relearns all dimensions. One realizes: land is vast, water is something big, and especially vast is the sky. What I had seen up to now was only a replica of land and river and world. Yet here, everything is the real thing.—I feel as if I had observed creation; few words for the totality of being, the things [presented] in the dimensions of God the Father. (*Tagebücher aus der Frühzeit*, 195–96)

Much of "The Book of Pilgrimage" is concerned with the right way of seeing things, including God. On September 1, 1900, Rilke writes in his diary: "Do you remember when I said: Well, everything that has really been seen must become poetry as a matter of course?" (196). He presumes since that has not been the case, he either has not observed properly or his creative output does not depend on the right way of observing, as he previously thought. Rilke does not resolve this question in his musings about his Russian journey. But he feels that the best things are yet to come.

> After all I have experienced it all, I certainly did more than dream. If only I could retrieve it. I have a great longing for the past. I do

not want to mull over it. But I would like to experience half con-
sciously [the past's] values of things. I will never stop being sad over
their loss. . . . To be awake and to live are activities. And I did not
do them. (198)

Four weeks later, September 27, Rilke records in his "Worp-
sweder Diary" the need to keep practicing the art of seeing as he
had learned from "these scrupulous and good painters that
come so incredibly close to images":

I must learn a lot more from these people, be attentive and awake
and more grateful toward all my surroundings. And a second thing
too: after Christmas I will have to go to Paris so as to view pictures,
visit Rodin, and catch up on so much that I have become estranged
from during my solitude. The Russian journey with its daily losses
is such a very sad testimony of my immature eyes, which do not
know how to receive, how to grasp and release; these eyes which,
stacked with tormenting images, pass by beauty only to walk toward
disappointments. (264)

And yet Rilke feels, despite his need to see better, that "all
forces" gather in him, that his language is rich, that he frequently
speaks of eternal things. And when he does in conversations
with others,

I can tell from their looks: I have said something great. I hope it
does not sound haughty, what I am saying—that it would rather
reflect deep gratitude on my part. But there are days when I cannot
talk about myself without talking about God, this lonely God, in
whose shadow my words grow dark and sparkle. (265)

Rilke, then, sees himself as more than someone who prays, like
the monk in "The Book of Pilgrimage": "For those who pray do

not talk about him. Perhaps I am more than one praying. Perhaps I have been commissioned to be a sort of priest; perhaps I am destined, alienated from others, to approach a person, festively as it were, as from golden doors" (296).

In this role of priest, rather than praying monastic and recluse, Rilke considers the aspect of God's becoming in reciprocity with people. People have perceived God as complete because they needed God fully developed. But now God has to catch up with the process of becoming. "We are the ones helping God to do so," Rilke says. "We cannot do anything that does not also affect Him, provided we have found ourselves first." This is then what Rilke concludes from his musings: "I have to be big so as to do justice to His greatness; I have to be simple so as not to confuse Him; I have to be serious so that my seriousness will come to meet His at some point" (295–96).

And yet, in spite of our crucial role in helping God become, Rilke is prompted, when asked by a young philosopher whether modern art believed in God, to recall "the great beauty of my Florentine days" and replies: "One knows that no one can do anything without [God]." Only much later, Rilke says, is he able to live this statement—a statement that initially startled him, "and do so better every day" (297).

"THE BOOK OF POVERTY AND DEATH"

Rilke wrote the third book of *The Book of Hours,* titled "The Book of Poverty and Death," between April 13 and 20, 1903, in Viareggio, Italy. The God of the monk seems far removed. Images of Eastern and Western art, the Russian landscape, monasteries, and pilgrims' sites are exchanged for images of the poor in large cities, coupled with allusions to the Italian Alps, St. Francis of Assisi, and possibly Orpheus.

The despised large cities cited in the book are most certainly Western cities, in particular Paris, where Rilke had moved in August 1902 so as to write a monograph on the sculptor Auguste Rodin. In a letter to Lou Andreas-Salomé, dated June 30, 1903, which was one of the first after she had broken off correspondence with him in February 1901, Rilke writes about Paris:

> The city was against me, opposed to my life, and like a test I failed. Her cry that never stopped broke into my quiet, her horror followed me into my sad living room, and my eyes lay heavy under the images of her days. (*Briefwechsel,* 45)

In comforting contrast stands Rilke's experience in Russia, with its vastness of land, simplicity of life, and the piety of the people and peasantry as suggested by the multitude of pilgrims and monasteries. In light of the merciless and deceptive cities that harbor death and seem to conceal God, the monk longs for the Eastern plains where God seemed ever present and apparent.

For Rilke it is easier to dream about his idealized Russia than to actually return and retrieve it and perhaps be disappointed with its reality. In the same way, the monk is invariably "sent" back to the big city. Rilke continues in the letter to Lou:

> The fear arose in me that my most dreadful hour might be in this other world from where I cannot leave so as to meet people. . . . Perhaps it [the fear] is only a consequence of this terrible and heavy city, for which I was way too soft and squeamish; perhaps these are the reflections of those fears resulting from our poverty: there were so many of them during the year in Westerwede and [now] here, where being poor and perishing are so similar. (48)

When Rilke refers to the year in Westerwede as being poor, he means it in both the literal and the symbolic sense. It was the year

1901, which saw the break with Lou, who had retreated in February, and where in March Rilke announced his engagement to the sculptor Clara Westhoff, whom he married on April 29, 1901. Rilke wrote in his diary that he wanted to help the "dear young girl" to an awareness of her greatness as an artist, while Lou thought that Rilke had been trapped, because Clara was pregnant at the time of the wedding. A daughter, Ruth, was born in November 1901. Rilke left for Paris ten months later, Clara shortly thereafter, leaving Ruth at her grandmother's. The couple lived in separate quarters—a sign of their early irreconcilable estrangement, though they remained on friendly terms with each other.

While Rilke had experienced the death of his marriage, he witnessed death in the daily life of the city: people who were dehumanized, robbed of hope and everything that made life bearable, even their dignity in dying. As a result, Rilke conceives of a valiant warrior, a sort of Nietzschean superman, who gives birth to death in its perfect form so as to allow others to benefit from and bear this new creature in their own right. The imagery is set in contrast with the Virgin Mary, who gives birth to new life in the form of the Christ child. Rilke's monk desires a counterpart that gives birth to Perfect Death through whom people can die in dignity, instead of being caught unawares or mangled by death in protracted illness. Rilke's personal stubborn resistance to allowing his physician to inform him of his illness, namely leukemia, parallels this sentiment.

The sexual imagery begun in the scene about the bearer of death continues and is linked with poverty in the appearance of St. Francis of Assisi. The book contains references to an episode of St. Francis's shedding his clothes, his denial of wealth, his attractiveness to the nuns as a spiritual bridegroom, his song, and the increasing recognition of his presence by all of nature. St. Francis becomes the idealized incarnation of poverty. Various commentators suggest that Rilke has subtly alternated between the appearance of St. Francis and Orpheus, the singer of eternal songs, addressed in Rilke's 1923 *Sonnets to Orpheus.*

While in the two earlier books Russia had been idealized as the place of God's presence, now God is in the midst of those that are poor. Four years prior to writing "The Book of Poverty and Death," Rilke had made reference to poverty in his "Florentine Diary," comparing poverty to a morning song.

> I wish God would allow our hands to become like our eyes: ready to let go, bright when holding on, careless in releasing all things; then we could indeed be rich. . . . Our hands are not to be a casket: only a bed, nursing [things] there while they are about to fall asleep and are dreaming and thus releasing their favorite secrets to us. And then, things are to journey on past these hands, sturdy and strong, and we should not keep anything of them, except the bold morning song that lingers and shines behind their echoing steps. For possessing is poverty and fear; only having possessed is unconcerned possessing. (*Tagebücher aus der Frühzeit,* 130)

The book ends with Poverty appearing at the end of the day, as if at life's end, as the great evening star. The future, becoming God whom the monk sought to assist and support in the two previous books, has now become the representation of, as well as presence among, those who are poor. The monk celebrates God's living among the poor. And because God does so, the poor are blessed.

SELECTED BIBLIOGRAPHY

Bly, Robert. *Selected Poems of Rainer Maria Rilke: A Translation from the German and Commentary.* New York: Harper and Row, 1981.

Brodsky, Patricia Pollock. *Russia in the Works of Rainer Maria Rilke.* Detroit: Wayne State University Press, 1984.

Hendry, J. F. *The Sacred Threshold: A Life of Rainer Maria Rilke.*
Manchester: Carcanet New Press, 1983.

Holthusen, Hans Egon. *Portrait of Rilke: An Illustrated Biography.*
Trans. W. H. Hargreaves. New York: Herder and Herder, 1971.

Mason, C. Eudo. "Introduction" in Rainer Maria Rilke, *The Book of
Hours.* Trans. A. L. Peck. London: Hogarth Press, 1961.

Mövius, Ruth. *Rainer Maria Rilkes Stunden-Buch: Entstehung und Gehalt.*
Leipzig: Insel Verlag, 1937.

Reshetylo-Rothe, Daria A. *Rilke and Russia: A Re-Evaluation.* New
York: Peter Lang, 1990.

Rilke, Rainer Maria. *Sämtliche Werke.* 7 vols. Ed. Ruth Rilke Sieber.
Frankfurt: Insel Verlag, 1955–97.

——. *Tagebücher aus der Frühzeit (1899–1902).* Eds. Ruth Rilke
Sieber and Carl Sieber. Leipzig: Insel Verlag, 1942.

Rilke, Rainer Maria, and Lou Andreas-Salomé. *Briefwechsel.* Ed. Ernst
Pfeiffer. Zürich: M. Niehaus, 1952.

Schnack, Ingeborg. *Rainer Maria Rilke: Chronik seines Lebens und seines
Werkes.* Frankfurt: Insel Verlag, 1996.

» The Book of Hours

ERSTES BUCH, 1899

Da neigt sich die Stunde und rührt mich an
mit klarem, metallenem Schlag:
mir zittern die Sinne. Ich fühle: ich kann—
und ich fasse den plastischen Tag.

Nichts war noch vollendet, eh ich es erschaut,
ein jedes Werden stand still.
Meine Blicke sind reif, und wie eine Braut
kommt jedem das Ding, das er will.

Nichts ist mir zu klein und ich lieb es trotzdem
und mal' es auf Goldgrund und groß
und halte es hoch, und ich weiß nicht wem
löst es die Seele los . . .

» » »

Ich lebe mein Leben ich wachsenden Ringen,
die sich über die Dinge ziehn.
Ich werde den letzten vielleicht nicht vollbringen,
aber versuchen will ich ihn.

Ich kreise um Gott, um den uralten Turm,
und ich kreise jahrtausendelang;
und ich weiß noch nicht: bin ich ein Falke, ein Sturm
oder ein großer Gesang.

»»» The Book of the Monkish Life

The clock has struck and nudges me
with clear and metallic beats:
My senses tremble. I feel I am able—
and I tackle the day that greets.

Not a thing had been finished of what I could see,
and any becoming stood still.
My vision is seasoned, and like a bride,
obtains just the thing it wills.

There's nothing too small, I can still find its charm
and paint it in gold and quite big,
I hold it up high without even knowing
whose soul will be fed by it . . .

» » »

I live my life in circles that grow;
upon it all their lines seem to press.
Though I may not manage the ultimate circle,
I will give it a try nonetheless.

I circle around God, around the tower of old,
and I spin amidst thousands of years;
yet unclear of my role, be it falcon or storm
or another magnificent song.

» » »

Ich habe viele Brüder in Soutanen
im Süden, wo in Klöstern Lorbeer steht.
Ich weiß, wie menschlich sie Madonnen planen,
und träume oft von jungen Tizianen,
durch die der Gott in Gluten geht.

Doch wie ich mich auch in mich selber neige:
Mein Gott ist dunkel und wie ein Gewebe
von hundert Wurzeln, welche schweigsam trinken.
Nur, daß ich mich aus *seiner* Wärme hebe,
mehr weiß ich nicht, weil alle meine Zweige
tief unten ruhn und nur im Winde winken.

» » »

Wir dürfen dich nicht eigenmächtig malen,
du Dämmernde, aus der der Morgen stieg.
Wir holen aus den alten Farbenschalen
die gleichen Striche und die gleichen Strahlen,
mit denen dich der Heilige verschwieg.

Wir bauen Bilder vor dir auf wie Wände;
so daß schon tausend Mauern um dich stehn.
Denn dich verhüllen unsre frommen Hände,
sooft dich unsre Herzen offen sehn.

» » »

Ich liebe meines Wesens Dunkelstunden,
in welchen meine Sinne sich vertiefen;

» » »

I have many brothers who are monks in the South
in abbeys with bayberry trees.
And I know how so lifelike they design their madonnas
and I dream about their Titians, through which
God Almighty marches in bliss.

And yet, regardless of much introspection,
the God *I* see stands tissuelike and dark
with many roots that drink in calm.
Just that I draw from him is all I know
for all my branches barely sway on top
and rest below.

» » »

We may not paint you of our own accord,
you Mother Dawn, whence mornings come.
From coloring cans of old we draw
the same contours and lines and rays
once used by saints to hide your face.

We stockpile images of you like walls
so that a thousand walls already hide
your face, and covered by our pious hands
each time our hearts are wide.

» » »

I love the hours when I'm blue, depressed,
my senses sharpened and I wide awake;

in ihnen hab ich, wie in alten Briefen,
mein täglich Leben schon gelebt gefunden
und wie Legende weit und überwunden.

Aus ihnen kommt mir Wissen, daß ich Raum
zu einem zweiten zeitlos breiten Leben habe.

Und manchmal bin ich wie der Baum,
der, reif und rauschend, über einem Grabe
den Traum erfüllt, den der vergangne Knabe
(um den sich seine warmen Wurzeln drängen)
verlor in Traurigkeiten und Gesängen.

» » »

Du, Nachbar Gott, wenn ich dich manches Mal
in langer Nacht mit hartem Klopfen störe,—
so ists, weil ich dich selten atmen höre
und weiß: Du bist allein im Saal.
Und wenn du etwas brauchst, ist keiner da,
um deinem Tasten einen Trank zu reichen:
Ich horche immer. Gib ein kleines Zeichen.
Ich bin ganz nah.

Nur eine schmale Wand ist zwischen uns,
durch Zufall; denn es könnte sein:
ein Rufen deines oder meines Munds—
und sie bricht ein
ganz ohne Lärm und Laut.

Aus deinen Bildern ist sie aufgebaut.

for then I have found, as in letters of late,
my future life lived out like stories
and lived out at best.

These hours give me assurance that I have
the room for a second, a much fuller life.

And sometimes I am like the tree
which, ripe and rustling above a grave,
fulfills himself the dream the boy
(round whom the living roots entwine)
once had and lost.

» » »

You, neighbor God, when I disturb with heavy raps
your quiet during a lonely night,
it is because I rarely hear you breathe,
though know: You're in your room alone.
And while in need, there's no one there to bring
your groping hand a drink. But I
am listening. Just give me a sign.
I am close by.

Only a thin wall is between us,
mere happenstance; so there is a chance
that a call from your or my mouth
might break it down
without sound.

The wall's building blocks are pictures of you.

Und deine Bilder stehn vor dir wie Namen.
Und wenn einmal das Licht in mir entbrennt,
mit welchem meine Tiefe dich erkennt,
vergeudet sichs als Glanz auf ihren Rahmen.

Und meine Sinne, welche schnell erlahmen,
sind ohne Heimat und von dir getrennt.

» » »

Wenn es nur einmal so ganz stille wäre.
Wenn das Zufällige und Ungefähre
verstummte und das nachbarliche Lachen,
wenn das Geräusch, das meine Sinne machen,
mich nicht so sehr verhinderte am Wachen—

Dann könnte ich in einem tausendfachen
Gedanken bis an deinen Rand dich denken
und dich besitzen (nur ein Lächeln lang),
um dich an alles Leben zu verschenken
wie einen Dank.

» » »

Ich lebe grad, da das Jahrhundert geht.
Man fühlt den Wind von einem großen Blatt,
das Gott und du und ich beschrieben hat
und das sich hoch in fremden Händen dreht.

Man fühlt den Glanz von einer neuen Seite,
auf der noch Alles werden kann.

And these pictures form shields like names.
And when at times the light in me comes on
and makes my soul conceive you as you are,
it wastes itself as glimmer on these pictures' frames.

But since my senses tend to tire quickly and grow lame,
they then grow homeless once again and we apart.

» » »

If only it were absolutely quiet here at times.
If averageness and happenstance grew silent
and the neighbor's laugh,
the noise my high-strung senses make
would not prevent my staying awake—

I could in one millennial thought
conceive you in your farthest reach
and could possess you (like a fleeting smile)
and dole you out as gifts with gratitude
to all of life.

» » »

I live on the verge of the century's turn.
One feels the wind as from a page,
which God, and you and I, have written on,
which spins above in hands unknown.

One catches the sheen of an empty page,
where everything new is yet to be.

Die stillen Kräfte prüfen ihre Breite
und sehn einander dunkel an.

》 》 》

Ich lese es heraus aus deinem Wort,
aus der Geschichte der Gebärden,
mit welchen deine Hände um das Werden
sich ründeten, begrenzend, warm und weise.
Du sagtest leben laut und sterben leise
und wiederholtest immer wieder: Sein.
Doch vor dem ersten Tode kam der Mord.
Da ging ein Riß durch deine reifen Kreise
und ging ein Schrein
und riß die Stimmen fort,
die eben erst sich sammelten,
um dich zu sagen,
um dich zu tragen
alles Abgrunds Brücke—

Und was sie seither stammelten,
sind Stücke
deines alten Namens.

》 》 》

Der blasse Abelknabe spricht:

Ich bin nicht. Der Bruder hat mir was getan,
was meine Augen nicht sahn.
Er hat mir das Licht verhängt.
Er hat mein Gesicht verdrängt

The silent forces test their breath
and face each other furiously.

» » »

I conclude it from your Word,
from your gestures of the past,
when you, hands cupped, limits set, gave rise
to all that is and was, so warm and wise.
You said "living" loud and "dying" low
and ever repeated: "Be."
But there came murder before the first death
And a sharp rip went through your circles so ripe
and a loud scream ran through
and tore the voices away
which had just assembled to speak
and talk about you and carry you high,
as bridge over any abyss.

And what they have been stammering since then
are but pieces
of your former name.

» » »

The pale Abel says:

I do not exist.
The brother has done what my eyes couldn't see.
He has covered up my light.
He has pushed my face away

mit seinem Gesicht.
Er ist jetzt allein.
Ich denke, er muß noch sein.
Denn ihm tut niemand, wie er mir getan.
Es gingen alle meine Bahn,
kommen alle vor seinen Zorn,
gehen alle an ihm verloren.

Ich glaube, mein großer Bruder wacht
wie ein Gericht.
An mich hat die Nacht gedacht;
an ihn nicht.

» » »

Du Dunkelheit, aus der ich stamme,
ich liebe dich mehr als die Flamme,
welche die Welt begrenzt,
indem sie glänzt
für irgend einen Kreis,
aus dem heraus kein Wesen von ihr weiß.

Aber die Dunkelheit hält alles an sich:
Gestalten und Flammen, Tiere und mich,
wie sie's errafft,
Menschen und Mächte—

Und es kann sein: eine große Kraft
rührt sich in meiner Nachbarschft.

Ich glaube an Nächte.

and replaced it with his.
Now he is alone.
I figure he is still alive.
For no one would dare do to him what he did to me.
Everybody will have to walk my path,
all will fall victim to his wrath,
all will be lost on him.

I believe my big brother is now forced
to watch like a court.
The night has remembered me,
but him not.

》 》 》

You darkness whence I came,
I love you more than the light
which marks the world's seam
by her gleaming for some orbit,
apart from which
no one knows who she is.

But the darkness holds it all in:
figures and flames, beasts and me,
whatever it may catch,
humans and rights—

It is possible that there might
be moving a power right next to me.

I believe in nights.

» » »

Ich glaube an Alles noch nie Gesagte.
Ich will meine frömmsten Gefühle befrein.
Was noch keiner zu wollen wagte,
wird mir einmal unwillkürlich sein.

Ist das vermessen, mein Gott, vergib.
Aber ich will dir damit nur sagen:
Meine beste Kraft soll sein wie ein Trieb,
so ohne Zürnen und ohne Zagen;
so haben dich ja die Kinder lieb.

Mit diesem Hinfluten, mit diesem Münden
in breiten Armen ins offene Meer,
mit dieser wachsenden Wiederkehr
will ich dich bekennen, will ich dich verkünden
wie keiner vorher.

Und ist das Hoffahrt, so laß mich hoffährtig sein
für mein Gebet,
das so ernst und allein
vor deiner wolkigen Stirne steht.

» » »

Ich bin auf der Welt zu allein und doch nicht allein
        genug,
um jede Stunde zu weihn.
Ich bin auf der Welt zu gering und doch nicht klein
        genug,
um vor dir zu sein wie ein Ding,

» » »

I believe in everything that's never been said.
My most pious thoughts I want to set free.
What no one has ever dared to desire
will come to me fortuitously.

If this be boasting, my Lord, forgive.
I only wanted to say that my talents should be
like a passion for which I live,
the same way the children love you so much—
free from anger or disbelief.

With this rushing and flowing and running
with widening banks into the open sea's door,
as during ever repeating rendezvous,
I want to profess and proclaim you
as no one before.

And if this be presumptuous so let it be
for the sake of my prayer,
which so earnestly and forlorn
lingers across your cloud-clad brow.

» » »

I am much too alone in this world, yet not alone
        enough
to truly consecrate the hour.
I am much too small in this world, yet not small
        enough
to be to you just object and thing,

dunkel und klug.
Ich will meinen Willen und will meinen Willen begleiten
die Wege zur Tat;
und will in stillen, irgenwie zögernden Zeiten,
wenn etwas naht,
unter den Wissenden sein
oder allein.

Ich will dich immer spiegeln in ganzer Gestalt,
und will niemals blind sein oder zu alt
um dein schweres schwankendes Bild zu halten.
Ich will mich entfalten.
Nirgends will ich gebogen bleiben,
denn dort bin ich gelogen, wo ich gebogen bin.
Und ich will meinen Sinn
wahr vor dir. Ich will mich beschreiben
wie ein Bild das ich sah,
lange und nah,
wie ein Wort, das ich begriff,
wie meinen täglichen Krug,
wie meiner Mutter Gesicht,
wie ein Schiff
das mich trug
durch den tödlichsten Sturm.

» » »

Du siehst, ich will viel.
Vielleicht will ich Alles:
das Dunkel jedes unendlichen Falles
und jedes Steigens lichtzitterndes Spiel.

dark and smart.
I want my free will and want it accompanying
the path which leads to action;
and want during times that beg questions,
where something is up,
to be among those in the know,
or else be alone.

I want to mirror your image to its fullest perfection,
never be blind or too old
to uphold your weighty wavering reflection.
I want to unfold.
Nowhere I wish to stay crooked, bent;
for there I would be dishonest, untrue.
I want my conscience to be
true before you;
want to describe myself like a picture I observed
for a long time, one close up,
like a new word I learned and embraced,
like the everyday jug,
like my mother's face,
like a ship that carried me along
through the deadliest storm.

» » »

You see I want much.
Perhaps I want it all:
the dark that goes with any bottomless fall
and the sun-speckled climbing up.

Es leben so viele und wollen nichts,
und sind durch ihres leichten Gerichts
glatte Gefühle gefürstet.

Aber du freust dich jedes Gesichts,
das dient und dürstet.

Du freust dich Aller, die dich gebrauchen
wie ein Gerät.

Noch bist du nicht kalt, und es ist nicht zu spät,
in deine werdenden Tiefen zu tauchen,
wo sich das Leben ruhig verrät.

» » »

Wir bauen an dir mit zitternden Händen
und wir türmen Atom auf Atom.
Aber wer kann dich vollenden,
du Dom.

Was ist Rom?
Es zerfällt.
Was ist die Welt?
Sie wird zerschlagen
eh deine Türme Kuppeln tragen,
eh aus Meilen von Mosaik
deine strahlende Stirne stieg.

Aber manchmal im Traum
kann ich deinen Raum
überschaun,

So many there are who don't want a thing,
who are dulled by their senses,
their easy weight.

But you are glad for every face
that seeks and serves.

You rejoice in those who apply you
like an instrument.

You haven't turned cold yet, it's not too late
to dive into your expanding depths,
where life reveals its intent.

» » »

We build on you with trembling hands
and we stack atom on atom.
But who can complete you,
you dome.

What is Rome?
It collapses.
What is the world?
It is destroyed
ere your towers carry cupolas,
ere out of mosaic-covered miles
emerges your gleaming face.

But sometimes in a dream
I can survey your room,
deep down where it had its start

tief vom Beginne
bis zu des Daches goldenem Grate.

Und ich seh: meine Sinne
bilden und baun
die letzten Zierate.

» » »

Daraus, daß Einer dich einmal gewollt hat,
weiß ich, daß wir dich wollen dürfen.
Wenn wir auch alle Tiefen verwürfen:
wenn ein Gebirge Gold hat
und keiner mehr es ergraben mag,
trägt es einmal der Fluß zutag,
der in die Stille der Steine greift,
der vollen.

Auch wenn wir nicht wollen:
Gott reift.

» » »

Wer seines Lebens viele Widersinne
versöhnt und dankbar in ein Sinnbild faßt,
der drängt
die Lärmenden aus dem Palast,
wird *anders* festlich, und du bist der Gast,
den er an sanften Abenden empfängt.

Du bist der Zweite seiner Einsamkeit,
die ruhige Mitte seinen Monologen;

all the way up to the roof,
under the cupola.

And I realize: my senses
are intent to fill in
the final trim.

» » »

Someone desired you once, which makes me know
it is permissible to long for you.
Though we may discard our search of old:
it is like the mountain with its veins hiding gold
yet where no one wants to dig anymore,
and where one day the river will wash it forth,
the one mining deep
amidst silent stones.

Though we may not like it:
God grows.

» » »

Whoever manages to reconcile
the many contradictions of his life,
and views them gratefully as one big theme,
will drive all noisemakers out of the house
and celebrate so differently at dusk
with you alone as guest.

You are the second one amidst your loneliness,
the quiet center of each monologue:

und jeder Kreis, um dich gezogen,
spannt ihm den Zirkel aus der Zeit.

» » »

Was irren meine Hände in den Pinseln?
Wenn ich dich *male,* Gott, du merkst es kaum.

Ich *fühle* dich. An meiner Sinne Saum
beginnst du zögernd, wie mit vielen Inseln,
und deinen Augen, welche niemals blinseln,
bin ich der Raum.

Du bist nichtmehr inmitten deines Glanzes,
wo alle Linien des Engeltanzes
die Fernen dir verbrauchen wie Musik,—
du wohnst in deinem allerletzten Haus.
Dein ganzer Himmel horcht in mich hinaus,
weil ich mich sinnend dir verschwieg.

» » »

Ich bin, du Ängstlicher. Hörst du mich nicht
mit allen meinen Sinnen an dir branden?
Meine Gefühle, welche Flügel fanden,
umkreisen weiß dein Angesicht.
Siehst du nicht meine Seele, wie sie dicht
vor dir in einem Kleid aus Stille steht?
Reift nicht mein mailiches Gebet
an deinem Blicke wie an einem Baum?

Wenn du der Träumer bist, bin ich dein Traum.
Doch wenn du wachen willst, bin ich dein Wille

and any circle drawn round you
exceeds the tent of time.

» » »

Why should my hands get lost in brushes?
For when I draw you, Lord, you'd hardly know of it.

I'd rather feel you. On my senses' hem
you gently start by dotting islands on a map,
and to your eyes which never blink or bat
I am the room.

You stand no longer in your glistening
with angels dancing, robbing you,
like music, of a broader view—
you live, instead, far back.
This sky of yours stands listening
for me since I withdrew.

» » »

I am, you timid one. Do you not hear
how my longing is washing against your ear?
My feelings, which grew angels' wings,
encircle you like down.
Do you not see my soul as it comes
up to you in its gown?
Does not my springtime prayer in degrees
ripen by my looking up?

If you are the dreamer, then I am the dream.
Yet if you wanted to stay awake,

und werde mächtig aller Herrlichkeit
und ründe mich wie eine Sternenstille
über der wunderlichen Stadt der Zeit.

» » »

Mein Leben ist nicht diese steile Stunde,
darin du mich so eilen siehst.
Ich bin ein Baum vor meinem Hintergrunde,
ich bin nur einer meiner vielen Munde
und jener, welcher sich am frühsten schließt.

Ich bin die Ruhe zwischen zweien Tönen,
die sich nur schlecht aneinander gewöhnen:
denn der Ton Tod will sich erhöhn—

Aber im dunklen Intervall versöhnen
sich beide zitternd.
                    Und das Licht bleibt schön.

» » »

Wenn ich gewachsen wäre irgendwo,
wo leichtere Tage sind und schlanke Stunden,
ich hätte dir ein großes Fest erfunden,
und meine Hände hielten dich nicht so,
wie sie dich manchmal halten, bang und hart.

Dort hätte ich gewagt, dich zu vergeuden,
du grenzenlose Gegenwart.
Wie einen Ball
hätt ich dich in alle wogenden Freuden

I would be your will and would take charge
of all your majesty and curl up like the stillness of stars
over this city called time.

》》》

My life is not made up of haste and hurry,
in which you see me so often engrossed.
I am a tree in my own backyard,
I am only one of my many mouths
and the one always first to close.

I am the peace between two sounds
that would rather swing alone:
the note named Death is always proud—

But at intermission in the dark
they reconcile, though hesitantly.
                    And the song stays intact.

》》》

If I had grown up some other place,
with shorter hours and easier days,
I would have invented a feast for you,
and my hands wouldn't hold you as they sometimes do,
so anxiously and uncouth.

There I would have dared to squander you,
you limitless present tense.
I would have thrown you like a ball
into any possible delight,

hineingeschleudert, daß einer dich finge
und deinem Fall
mit hohen Händen entgegenspringe,
du Ding der Dinge.

Ich hätt dich wie eine Klinge
blitzen lassen.
Vom goldensten Ringe
ließ ich dein Feuer umfassen,
und er müßte mirs halten
über die weißeste Hand.

Gemalt hätt ich dich: nicht an die Wand,
an den Himmel selber von Rand zu Rand,
und hätt dich gebildet, wie ein Gigant
dich bilden würde: als Berg, als Brand,
als Samum, wachsend aus Wüstensand—

oder
es kann auch sein: ich fand
dich einmal . . .
            Meine Freunde sind weit,
ich höre kaum noch ihr Lachen schallen;
und du: du bist aus dem Nest gefallen,
bist ein junger Vogel mit gelben Krallen
und großen Augen und tust mir leid.
(Meine Hand ist dir viel zu breit.)
Und ich heb mit dem Finger vom Quell einen Tropfen
und lausche, ob du ihn lechzend langst,
und ich fühle dein Herz und meines klopfen
und beide aus Angst.

and somebody would catch and brace your fall
with outstretched and lifted hands,
you thing of things,
you all in all.

I would have let you shine
like the blade of a knife.
I would mount your fire
on the most golden of rings,
which would have to hold it
over the whitest of hands.

I would have painted you: not on the wall
but unto heaven itself;
would have sculpted you like a genius would:
as mountain, as fire, as seed so round
grown from the desert's sand.

Or
it might be that I found
you once . . .
        My friends are away and far,
so that I can barely remember their laugh:
And you, it seems, fell out of your nest,
like a young bird with yellow claws
and eyes that cause pity in my chest.
(My hand is so big next to you.)
And I lift with my finger a drop from a spring;
that you lap it up is what I want to hear,
and I feel your heart beat and mine too
out of fear.

» » »

Ich finde dich in allen diesen Dingen,
denen ich gut und wie ein Bruder bin;
als Samen sonnst du dich in den geringen
und in den großen gibst du groß dich hin.

Das ist das wundersame Spiel der Kräfte,
daß sie so dienend durch die Dinge gehn:
in Wurzeln wachsend, schwindend in die Schäfte
und in den Wipfeln wie ein Auferstehn.

» » »

Stimme eines jungen Bruders

Ich verrinne, ich verrinne
wie Sand, der durch Finger rinnt.
Ich habe auf einmal so viele Sinne,
die alle anders durstig sind.
Ich fühle mich an hundert Stellen
schwellen und schmerzen.
Aber am meisten mitten im Herzen.

Ich möchte sterben. Laß mich allein.
Ich glaube, es wird mir gelingen,
so bange zu sein,
daß mir die Pulse zerspringen.

» » »

Sieh, Gott, es kommt ein Neuer an dir bauen,
der gestern noch ein Knabe war; von Frauen

»　»　»

I find you in all these things to which I'm close,
to whom I'm brother;
as seed you take glory in all that is small
and among the great you offer your greatness to others.

This is the miraculous play of the forces,
that they rush as servants through the veins of life:
they grow in their roots, disappear into stems
and rise up atop as new life.

»　»　»

Voice of a young brother

I am hastily wasting away
like sand running through hands.
I have at once so many senses
with such a different appetite.
I feel that I'm hurting in a hundred places,
they swell and smart,
but the most in my heart.

I want to die. Leave me alone.
I think it possible for me to hurt
so much that my wrists
on their own will burst.

»　»　»

See, God, there's another one working on you,
who was just a boy yesterday;

sind seine Hände noch zusammengefügt
zu einem Falten, welches halb schon lügt.
Denn seine Rechte will schon von der Linken,
um sich zu wehren oder um zu winken
und um am Arm allein zu sein.

Noch gestern war die Stirne wie ein Stein
im Bach, geründet von den Tagen,
die nichts bedeuten als ein Wellenschlagen
und nichts verlangen, als ein Bild zu tragen
von Himmeln, die der Zufall drüber hängt;
heut drängt
auf ihr sich eine Weltgeschichte
vor einem unerbittlichen Gerichte,
und sie versinkt in seinem Urteilsspruch.

Raum wird auf einem neuen Angesichte.
Es war kein Licht vor diesem Lichte,
und, wie noch nie, beginnt dein Buch.

» » »

Ich liebe dich, du sanftestes Gesetz,
an dem wir reiften, da wir mit ihm rangen;
du großes Heimweh, das wir nicht bezwangen,
du Wald, aus dem wir nie hinausgegangen,
du Lied, das wir mit jedem Schweigen sangen,
du dunkles Netz,
darin sich flüchtend die Gefühle fangen.

Du hast dich so unendlich groß begonnen
an jenem Tage, da du uns begannst,—

with his hands still folded by women as if to pray
a prayer that's almost a lie.
For his right hand struggles to be free of the left,
in order to fight for its right or to wave,
and to be alone on its arm.

Only yesterday his brow was like a stone
in the creek, by daily ripples smoothed round,
by days that are nothing but wasted waves
and do not demand much but to carry
a reflection of the sky above;
but today the world's history crowds
his forehead out
and is submerged
by the verdict of its court.

Then there's room for another face
for a light that's never been there before,
and your story begins anew.

» » »

I love you, you the gentlest law
through which we ripen as we fight with it;
you homesickness we cannot quite curtail,
you forest within which we lose our trail,
you song we have sung with every silence kept,
you darkened net,
where every feeling apt to flee is caught.

You started out so infinitely great
when you began the day by making us—

und wir sind so gereift in deinen Sonnen,
so breit geworden und so tief gepflanzt,
daß du in Menschen, Engeln und Madonnen
dich ruhend jetzt vollenden kannst.

Laß deine Hand am Hang der Himmel ruhn
und dulde stumm, was wir dir dunkel tun.

» » »

Werkleute sind wir: Knappen, Jünger, Meister,
und bauen dich, du hohes Mittelschiff.
Und manchmal kommt ein ernster Hergereister,
geht wie ein Glanz durch unsre hundert Geister
und zeigt uns zitternd einen neuen Griff.

Wir steigen in die wiegenden Gerüste,
in unsern Händen hängt der Hammer schwer,
bis eine Stunde uns die Stirnen küßte,
die strahlend und als ob sie Alles wüßte
von dir kommt, wie der Wind vom Meer.

Dann ist ein Hallen von dem vielen Hämmern
und durch die Berge geht es Stoß um Stoß.
Erst wenn es dunkelt lassen wir dich los:
Und deine kommenden Konturen dämmern.

Gott, du bist groß.

» » »

and we became so ripened by your light
and grew so wide with roots that dug so deep,
so that in leisure now you can perfect yourself,
in virgins, angels, and in human selves.

O let your hand find rest on heaven's span
enduring patiently when we again offend.

》 》 》

Craftsmen we are, as novice, meddler, master,
who build you up, you tallest middle ship.
And sometimes drops a passing traveler by
who casts amidst our souls a passing ray
and humbly leaves with us another craftsman's trick.

We climb unto the swaying scaffolding;
in our hand the hammer hangs quite low
until a certain hour kisses our brow,
which radiates as if she knew it all
and comes from thee like wind from sea.

Then one hears echoes from the many hammers
and through the rocky mountains they pound knock
    by knock.
Not until dusk will our grips abate:
and your emerging contours dawn on us.

God, you are great.

》 》 》

Du bist so groß, daß ich schon nicht mehr bin,
wenn ich mich nur in deine Nähe stelle.
Du bist so dunkel; meine kleine Helle
an deinem Saum hat keinen Sinn.
Dein Wille geht wie eine Welle
und jeder Tag ertrinkt darin.

Nur meine Sehnsucht ragt dir bis ans Kinn
und steht vor dir wie aller Engel größter:
ein fremder, bleicher und noch unerlöster,
und hält dir seine Flügel hin.

Er will nicht mehr den uferlosen Flug,
an dem die Monde blaß vorüberschwammen,
und von den Welten weiß er längst genug.
Mit seinen Flügeln will er wie mit Flammen
vor deinem schattigen Gesichte stehn
und will bei ihrem weißen Scheine sehn,
ob deine grauen Brauen ihn verdammen.

» » »

So viele Engel suchen dich im Lichte
und stoßen mit den Stirnen nach den Sternen
und wollen dich aus jedem Glanze lernen.
Mir aber ist, sooft ich von dir dichte,
daß ich mit abgewendetem Gesichte
von deines Mantels Falten sich entfernen.

Denn du warst selber nur ein Gast des Golds.
Nur einer Zeit zuliebe, die dich flehte
in ihre klaren marmornen Gebete,

You are so great that I'm no longer me
the minute that I draw up close.
You are so dark; my little light grows dim
nearby your garment's folds.
Your will wafts like a wave
and every day is drenched in it.

Only my yearning tries to reach your chin
and looms as large as of the angel's tallest:
It's me, so strange and pale and unredeemed,
who offers you his wings.

For I no longer want the vast and endless flight
with moons grown pale and skipping by;
for what I know of worlds is good enough.
And with my wings I want to be like flames
that come before your darkened face
and help me see by their white glow
if I still stand accused by you.

》》》

So many angels seek you where the light is
and turn their heads toward the stars
and want to glean you in just any gleam.
To me it seems, however, anytime
I write of you in poetry and rhyme,
that they have made a turn away from you.

For you were only guest amidst the golden gleam yourself,
appearing just to please a pleading time
as prayer clear and marblelike,

erschienst du wie der König der Komete,
auf deiner Stirne Strahlenströme stolz.

Du kehrtest heim, da jene Zeit zerschmolz.

Ganz dunkel ist dein Mund, von dem ich wehte,
und deine Hände sind von Ebenholz.

» » »

Das waren Tage Michelangelo's,
von denen ich in fremden Büchern las.
Das war der Mann, der über einem Maß,
gigantengroß,
die Unermeßlichkeit vergaß.

Das war der Mann, der immer wiederkehrt,
wenn eine Zeit noch einmal ihren Wert,
da sie sich enden will, zusammenfaßt.
Da hebt noch einer ihre ganze Last
und wirft sie in den Abgrund seiner Brust.

Die vor ihm hatten Leid und Lust;
er aber fühlt nur noch des Lebens Masse
und daß er Alles wie *ein* Ding umfasse,—
nur Gott bleibt über seinem Willen weit:
da liebt er ihn mit seinem hohen Hasse
für diese Unerreichbarkeit.

» » »

Der Ast vom Baume Gott, der über Italien reicht,
hat schon geblüht.

as king of comets, proud you rode
amidst your rays of light.

But once this pleading time was passed—

You went back home. And now your mouth
and hands are ebony dark.

》 》 》

These were the days of Michelangelo
of which I read in foreign books.
This was the man who with a measuring tape,
enormously and great, ignored
immeasurability.

It is the man who, at each epoch's end,
returns to summarize
the era's benefit and its bequest;
as when one lifts each epoch's total weight
and throws it in the depths of his famed chest.

The ones before him only knew of pain and joy;
but he can feel the central theme of life
and seeks to see it all as one—despite
this God remaining far away from him; so he,
in mixed emotions of awed hate,
loves God for his unreachability.

》 》 》

The branch on God's tree spanning Italy
has bloomed already;

Er hätte vielleicht
sich schon gerne, mit Früchten gefüllt, verfrüht,
doch er wurde mitten im Blühen müd,
und er wird keine Früchte haben.

Nur der Frühling Gottes war dort,
nur sein Sohn, das Wort,
vollendete sich.
Es wendete sich
alle Kraft zu dem strahlenden Knaben.
Alle kamen mit Gaben
zu ihm;
alle sangen wie Cherubim
seinen Preis.

Und er duftete leis
als Rose der Rosen.
Er war ein Kreis
um die Heimatlosen.
Er ging in Mänteln und Metamorphosen
durch alle steigenden Stimmen der Zeit.

》 》 》

Da ward auch die zur Frucht Erweckte,
die schüchterne und schönerschreckte,
die heimgesuchte Magd geliebt.
Die Blühende, die Unentdeckte,
in der es hundert Wege gibt.

Da ließen sie sie gehn und schweben
und treiben mit dem jungen Jahr;

perhaps it would have longed
to bear fruit early on,
but grew tired of blooming
and bore no fruit at all.

Only God's spring season arrived there,
perfected everywhere
through his Son, the Word.
Everyone turned his eye
to the radiant boy.
All came with gifts to him;
all sang like cherubim
to his praise.

He was fragrant
like the rose of roses.
He was shelter
to the lost and homeless.
In mantles of bliss,
of metamorphosis,
he passed through the tempers of time.

» » »

And then there was the shy and shaken maid
who was waked and visited and, though afraid,
was loved into giving birth:
She the blossoming one,
with more paths than one, was discovered.

And they made her walk and hover
and float through the ages of time;

ihr dienendes Marien-Leben
ward königlich und wunderbar.
Wie feiertägliches Geläute
ging es durch alle Häuser groß;
und die einst mädchenhaft Zerstreute
war so versenkt in ihren Schooß
und so erfüllt von jenem Einen
und so für Tausende genug,
daß alles schien, sie zu bescheinen,
die wie ein Weinberg war und trug.

» » »

Aber als hätte die Last der Fruchtgehänge
und der Verfall der Säulen und Bogengänge
und der Abgesang der Gesänge
sie beschwert,
hat die Jungfrau sich in anderen Stunden,
wie von Größerem noch unentbunden,
kommenden Wunden
zugekehrt.

Ihre Hände, die sich lautlos lösten,
liegen leer.
Wehe, sie gebar noch nicht den Größten.
Und die Engel, die nicht trösten,
stehen fremd und furchtbar um sie her.

» » »

So hat man sie gemalt; vor allem Einer,
der seine Sehnsucht aus der Sonne trug.
Ihm reifte sie aus allen Rätseln reiner,

and her life as the handmaiden Mary
became majestic and divine.
Like the bells ringing on holidays,
her story rang in every house
and the once so girllike and distraught
became immersed in the thought
of the one whom she birthed
in ways fulfilling to all;
she, who as a vineyard yielded wine,
then drew, it seemed, all praise sublime.

» » »

But then, as if the burden of too much fruit
and the crumbling of pillars and archways above
and the abating of song
grew too heavy ere long,
the Virgin turned in her later hours
away from her even greater powers
and toward impending pain.

Her hands that had loosened in silence their hold
lie empty. Woe to her if she didn't bear
the greatest.
And the angels around her withhold
their care, acting cold.

» » »

Thus one has painted her: especially one
who carried his passion away from the sun.
To him she emerged ever more pure and plain,

aber im Leiden immer allgemeiner:
sein ganzes Leben war er wie ein Weiner,
dem sich das Weinen in die Hände schlug.

Er ist der schönste Schleier ihrer Schmerzen,
der sich an ihre wehen Lippen schmiegt,
sich über ihnen fast zum Lächeln biegt—
und von dem Licht aus sieben Engelskerzen
wird sein Geheimnis nicht besiegt.

» » »

Mit einem Ast, der jenem niemals glich,
wird Gott, der Baum, auch einmal sommerlich
verkündend werden und aus Reife rauschen;
in einem Lande, wo die Menschen lauschen,
wo jeder ähnlich einsam ist wie ich.

Denn nur dem Einsamen wird offenbart,
und vielen Einsamen der gleichen Art
wird mehr gegeben als dem schmalen Einen.
Denn jedem wird ein andrer Gott erscheinen,
bis sie erkennen, nah am Weinen,
daß durch ihr meilenweites Meinen,
durch ihr Vernehmen und Verneinen,
verschieden nur in hundert Seinen
ein Gott wie eine Welle geht.

Das ist das endlichste Gebet,
das dann die Sehenden sich sagen:
Die Wurzel Gott hat Frucht getragen,
geht hin, die Glocken zu zerschlagen;

but ever more inclusive in her pain:
All of his life he too was in tears and cries
until they touched upon his hands and dyes.

He is the fairest veil of her distress,
who sidles up against her smarting lips,
who bends around them almost into smiles—
and even light from seven candles tall
cannot unearth the secret that he hides.

》 》 》

Through just one branch which hardly looks like him
is God, the tree, proclaimed at last like spring,
and rustles with maturity amidst a land
where people listen rather carefully—
each one alone like me.

For only to the lonely revelation comes
and many lonely of a similar type
will fathom more than one.
For God appears to each a different way,
until they start to realize, near tears,
that through their mile-long musing
through their rejecting and concluding
that's nuanced only in their meanings
one God meanders under them.

This is the ultimate prayer, then,
which the seeing amidst themselves exchange:
the root called God has borne its fruit,
go hence to crash the tolling bells;

wir kommen zu den stillern Tagen,
in denen reif die Stunde steht.
Die Wurzel Gott hat Frucht getragen.
Seid ernst und seht.

» » »

Ich kann nicht glauben, daß der kleine Tod,
dem wir doch täglich übern Scheitel schaun,
uns eine Sorge bleibt und eine Not.

Ich kann nicht glauben, daß er ernsthaft droht;
ich lebe noch, ich habe Zeit zu bauen:
mein Blut ist länger als die Rosen rot.

Mein Sinn ist tiefer als das witzige Spiel
mit unsrer Furcht, darin er sich gefällt.
Ich bin die Welt,
aus der er irrend fiel.

                       Wie er
kreisende Mönche wandern so umher;
man fürchtet sich vor ihrer Wiederkehr,
man weiß nicht: ist es jedesmal derselbe,
sinds zwei, sinds zehn, sinds tausend oder mehr?
Man kennt nur diese fremde gelbe Hand,
die sich ausstreckt so nackt und nah—
da da:
als käm sie aus dem eigenen Gewand.

» » »

we've reached the quieter of days,
with the hour now complete.
The root called God has borne its fruit.
Be serious now and see.

» » »

I can't believe something small like death
over whose head we daily gaze
looks worrisome to us and grave.

I can't believe this death spells dread;
I'm still alive, have time to build;
my blood is older than a rose stays red.

My wits are sharper than the funny game
he plays so gleefully with our fear.
I am the world from which
he, now nonplussed, was ditched.

                              He is
just like those peripatetic monks
whose return one rather loathes;
where one doesn't know is it always the same,
or is it two, or ten, or a thousand, or more?
And one recognizes this strange yellow hand,
which reaches forth so naked and near—
there, there:
as if out of one's own coat.

» » »

Was wirst du tun, Gott, wenn ich sterbe?
Ich bin dein Krug (wenn ich zerscherbe?)
Ich bin dein Trank (wenn ich verderbe?)
Bin dein Gewand und dein Gewerbe,
mit mir verlierst du deinen Sinn.

Nach mir hast du kein Haus, darin
dich Worte, nah und warm, begrüßen.
Es fällt von deinen müden Füßen
die Samtsandale, die ich bin.

Dein großer Mantel läßt dich los.
Dein Blick, den ich mit meiner Wange
warm, wie mit einem Pfühl, empfange,
wird kommen, wird mich suchen, lange—
und legt beim Sonnenuntergange
sich fremden Steinen in den Schooß.

Was wirst du tun, Gott? Ich bin bange.

» » »

Du bist der raunende Verrußte,
auf allen Öfen schläfst du breit.
Das Wissen ist nur in der Zeit.
Du bist der dunkle Unbewußte
von Ewigkeit zu Ewigkeit.

Du bist der Bittende und Bange,
der aller Dinge Sinn beschwert.
Du bist die Silbe im Gesange,
die immer zitternder im Zwange
der starken Stimmen wiederkehrt.

What will you do, God, when I'm dead?
I am your pot (when I crash into potsherds?)
I am your drink (when I go bad?)
I am your cloak and your career;
without me you end up losing making sense.

After me your house will be gone from where
warm and kindred words came to greet.
And from your tired feet there drops
the velvet slipper which is me.

Your giant cloak releases you.
Your gaze I used to capture with my cheek,
as with a pillow in between,
will wander, searching me for long—
at dusk will finally settle on
a distant slab of rock.

I fret about you, God.

» » »

You are the whispering sooty one;
outstretched on every stove you lie.
With time alone all knowledge rests.
You are this dark subconsciousness,
from ever to evermore.

You are the pleading worried one,
who lends all things a deeper sense.
You are the syllable in song
which trembles first, but then returns
by force of voices strong.

Du hast dich anders nie gelehrt:

Denn du bist nicht der Schönumscharte,
um welchen sich der Reichtum reiht.
Du bist der Schlichte, welcher sparte.
Du bist der Bauer mit dem Barte
von Ewigkeit zu Ewigkeit.

» » »

An den jungen Bruder

Du, gestern Knabe, dem die Wirrnis kam:
Daß sich dein Blut in Blindheit nicht vergeude.
Du meinst nicht den Genuß, du meinst die Freude;
du bist gebildet als ein Bräutigam,
und deine Braut soll werden: deine Scham.

Die große Lust hat auch nach dir Verlangen,
und alle Arme sind auf einmal nackt.
Auf frommen Bildern sind die bleichen Wangen
von fremden Feuern überflackt;
und deine Sinne sind wie viele Schlangen,
die von des Tones Rot umfangen,
sich spannen in der Tamburine Takt.

Und plötzlich bist du ganz allein gelassen
mit deinen Händen, die dich hassen—
und wenn dein Wille nicht ein Wunder tut:

———————————————————

Another face you never wore:

You are not Popularity,
which draws a wealthy crowd about.
You are the frugal one who saves.
You are the farmer with the beard
from ever to evermore.

» » »

To the young monk

You stand perplexed, a barely grown boy:
Watch that your passion not be frittered away.
You know not to seek out pleasure, but joy;
for the high office of groom you've been named,
and your future bride is your shame.

The great desire pulls you in,
an arm appears all bare in a flash.
On pious paintings even cheeks once pale
turn crimson red with strange appeal;
desire twists like snakes in the sun,
reflecting its red in various shades,
and is taut to the beat of the drum.

And suddenly you are left alone as a man
with your two hands that hate you now so—
given your will wrought a miracle then:

_____

Aber da gehen wie durch dunkle Gassen
von Gott Gerüchte durch dein dunkles Blut.

» » »

An den jungen Bruder

Dann bete du, wie es dich dieser lehrt,
der selber aus der Wirrnis wiederkehrt
und so, daß er zu heiligen Gestalten,
die alle ihres Wesens Würde halten,
in einer Kirche und auf goldnen Smalten
die Schönheit malte, und sie hielt ein Schwert.

Er lehrt dich sagen:
        Du mein tiefer Sinn,
vertraue mir, daß ich dich nicht enttäusche;
in meinem Blute sind so viel Geräusche,
ich aber weiß, daß ich aus Sehnsucht bin.

Ein großer Ernst bricht über mich herein.
In seinem Schatten ist das Leben kühl.
Ich bin zum erstenmal mit dir allein,
du, mein Gefühl.
Du bist so mädchenhaft.
Es war ein Weib in meiner Nachbarschaft
und winkte mir aus welkenden Gewändern.
Du aber sprichst mir von so fernen Ländern.
Und meine Kraft
schaut nach den Hügelrändern.

» » »

And there come rushing from dark corridors
through your veins the rumors of God.

» » »

To the young monk

Then pray the way you were taught, as one
returning home from temptation, borne
in a way that honors the godly saints,
who all maintained their dignity;
in a way that paints, in a church or on a page,
beauty which carries a sword.

Then pray as one who learned to say:
                    O you, my deepest soul,
place trust in me so I will not displease you;
within my blood runs rampant dreadful din;
I know this longing I hold in.

A serious spell comes over me.
Within its shadow life is cold.
It's for the first time that I meet
with you, my feeling, maidenlike;
you, woman in my neighborhood
who waved at me from wilting wear.
But you, God, tell of distant lands,
so that my concentrated gaze
runs past the rolling hills.

» » »

Ich habe Hymnen, die ich schweige.
Es gibt ein Aufgerichtetsein,
darin ich meine Sinne neige:
du siehst mich groß und ich bin klein.
Du kannst mich dunkel unterscheiden
von jenen Dingen, welche knien;
sie sind wie Herden und sie weiden,
ich bin der Hirt am Hang der Heiden,
vor welchem sie zu Abend ziehn.
Dann komm ich hinter ihnen her
und höre dumpf die dunklen Brücken,
und in dem Rauch von ihren Rücken
verbirgt sich meine Wiederkehr.

» » »

Gott, wie begreif ich deine Stunde,
als du, daß sie im Raum sich runde,
die Stimme vor dich hingestellt;
dir war das Nichts wie eine Wunde,
da kühltest du sie mit der Welt.

Jetzt heilt es leise unter uns.

Denn die Vergangenheiten tranken
die vielen Fieber aus den Kranken,
wir fühlen schon in sanftem Schwanken
den ruhigen Puls des Hintergrunds.

Wir liegen lindernd auf dem Nichts
und wir verhüllen alle Risse;
du aber wächst ins Ungewisse
im Schatten deines Angesichts.

I have hymns that I keep to myself.
To an upward gaze within I bow my head:
You see me being straight and tall,
but I am small.
You can distinguish me aright
from things that kneel; from these
that are like sheep and graze.
I am the shepherd before those
who walk from hills of heather home.
There I follow from behind
and vaguely notice the bridges black,
and in the cloud that trails their backs
lives subtly my return.

» » »

O God, how do I grasp your life
as that which makes the hour full,
as voice that's placed ahead of you;
for nothingness, this painful sensation
to you, you eased with creation.

Now healing takes place among us.

Past tenses drank up in full
the many fevers of the sick.
We already sense in a gentle sway
the background's quiet beat.

We lie on nothingness so soothingly
and we conceal all tears and rips;
yet you become uncertainty,
your face still more eclipsed.

» » »

Alle, die ihre Hände regen
nicht in der Zeit, der armen Stadt,
all, die sie an Leises legen,
an eine Stelle, fern den Wegen,
die kaum noch einen Namen hat,—
sprechen dich aus, du Alltagssegen,
und sagen sanft auf einem Blatt:

Es gibt im Grunde nur Gebete,
so sind die Hände uns geweiht,
daß sie nichts schufen, was nicht flehte;
ob einer malte oder mähte,
schon aus dem Ringen der Geräte
entfaltete sich Frömmigkeit.

Die Zeit ist eine vielgestalte.
Wir hören manchmal von der Zeit,
und tun das Ewige und Alte;
wir wissen, daß uns Gott umwallte
groß wie ein Bart und wie ein Kleid.
Wir sind wie Adern im Basalte
in Gottes harter Herrlichkeit.

» » »

Der Name ist uns wie ein Licht
hart an die Stirn gestellt.
Da senkte sich mein Angesicht
vor diesem zeitigen Gericht
und sah (von dem es seither spricht)

》》》

All who are apt to fold their hands
apart from this life—this city so poor;
all who place them on quiet things,
upon a spot far from the path
that hardly could retain its name—
they spell you out, you daily grace,
and gently write upon a page:

Basically only prayer exists;
our hands have been anointed for this
and nothing they made did not supplicate;
whether one painted or mowed,
from the striving of each tool
did piety evolve.

This time appears in many shapes.
At times we hear time nudging us
and do what is, has always been.
We know that God enveloped us,
big as a beard and like a dress.
We are the lobes in lava rock
within the rock-hard bliss of God.

》》》

The name we bear is like a light
that's placed against our forehead hard.
But then my head dropped low—
before this early judgment call
and saw (what it still talks about)

dich, großes dunkelndes Gewicht
an mir und an der Welt.

Du bogst mich langsam aus der Zeit,
in die ich schwankend stieg;
ich neigte mich nach leisem Streit:
jetzt dauert deine Dunkelheit
um deinen sanften Sieg.

Jetzt hast du mich und weißt nicht wen,
denn deine breiten Sinne sehn
nur, daß ich dunkel ward.
Du hältst mich seltsam zart
und horchst, wie meine Hände gehn
durch deinen alten Bart.

» » »

Dein allererstes Wort war: *Licht:*
da ward die Zeit. Dann schwiegst du lange.
Dein zweites Wort ward Mensch und bange
(wir dunkeln noch in seinem Klange)
und wieder sinnt dein Angesicht.

Ich aber will dein drittes nicht.

Ich bete nachts oft: Sei der Stumme,
der wachsend in Gebärden bleibt
und den der Geist im Traume treibt,
daß er des Schweigens schwere Summe
in Stirnen und Gebirge schreibt.

you, great and overshadowing weight,
on me and on the world.

You slowly peeled me out of time;
I swayingly stepped into it
and yielded after subtle fights:
but now your darkling presence grieves
your gentle victory.

You conquered me and know me not,
for your far-reaching senses see
that within me was dark.
So strangely soft you cradle me
and listen how my hands run through
your old and grizzled beard.

» » »

Your very first decree was: Light;
thus time emerged. And you were quiet.
Your second one was man and fear
(we still are pained by what we hear)
and then again you stopped.

Your third one I want not.

At night I pray: Remain the mute
who silently unfolds in deeds,
who of himself keeps on proceeding,
etching weighty mounts of silence
unto mountains and countenances.

Sei du die Zuflucht vor dem Zorne,
der das Unsagbare verstieß.
Es wurde Nacht im Paradies:
sei du der Hüter mit dem Horne,
und man erzählt nur, daß er blies.

» » »

Du kommst und gehst. Die Türen fallen
viel sanfter zu, fast ohne Wehn.
Du bist der Leiseste von Allen,
die durch die leisen Häuser gehn.

Man kann sich so an dich gewöhnen,
daß man nicht aus dem Buche schaut,
wenn seine Bilder sich verschönen,
von deinem Schatten überblaut;
weil dich die Dinger immer tönen,
nur einmal leis und einmal laut.

Oft wenn ich dich in Sinnen sehe,
verteilt sich deine Allgestalt:
du gehst wie lauter lichte Rehe
und ich bin dunkel und bin Wald.

Du bist ein Rad, an dem ich stehe:
von deinen vielen dunklen Achsen
wird immer wieder eine schwer
und dreht sich näher zu mir her,
und meine willigen Werke wachsen
von Wiederkehr zu Wiederkehr.

You be the refuge from the wrath,
who exiled the unspeakable,
who made it night in Paradise;
you be the guardian with the horn
of whom one only says he blew.

» » »

You come and go. The portals swing
more gently shut, hardly a twinge.
You are the quietest of those
who visit peaceful homes.

It is easy getting used to you,
to keep one's head inside your book
with pictures ever more ornate
steeped in the bluish shade you shed;
for everything reflects your hues,
at times so bright, at times sedate.

When I conceive of you at times,
your all-embracing shape expands:
You stride like many lighted does
and I am dark and wooded lands.

You are the wheel by which I stand:
of all your many spokes there moves
repeatedly one close to me,
approaches me as from afar
so that my love to labor grows
from one time to the next.

» » »

Du bist der Tiefste, welcher ragte,
der Taucher und der Türme Neid.
Du bist der Sanfte, der sich sagte,
und doch: wenn dich ein Feiger fragte,
so schwelgtest du in Schweigsamkeit.

Du bist der Wald der Widersprüche.
Ich darf dich wiegen wie ein Kind,
und doch vollziehn sich deine Flüche,
die über Völkern furchtbar sind.

Dir ward das erste Buch geschrieben,
das erste Bild versuchte dich,
du warst im Leiden und im Lieben,
dein Ernst war wie aus Erz getrieben
auf jeder Stirn, die mit den sieben
erfüllten Tagen dich verglich.

Du gingst in Tausenden verloren,
und alle Opfer wurden kalt;
bis du in hohen Kirchenchoren
dich rührtest hinter goldnen Toren;
und eine Bangnis, die geboren,
umgürtete dich mit Gestalt.

» » »

Ich weiß: Du bist der Rätselhafte,
um den die Zeit in Zögern stand.
O wie so schön ich dich erschaffte

» » »

You are the deepest, who looms tall,
the diver and each tower's goal.
You are the gentle one who keeps,
in spite of cowards mocking you,
his tongue and arm in check.

You are the woods of paradox.
Though I may rock you like a child,
your curses ever come to pass
as dread on people's backs.

For you the first of books was named;
the earliest image sought you out.
You lived amidst all pain and love,
Your seriousness was iron cast
on every forehead that retrieved
your image in the world.

You disappeared amidst the crowds
and offerings you refused to touch;
until you stirred in choir lofts,
from far behind the gilded gates;
and a deep longing thereby born
became the outline of your form.

» » »

I know you are the rebuslike
round whom this age in waiting stands.
O how I beautifully draped you

in einer Stunde, die mich straffte,
in einer Hoffahrt meiner Hand.

Ich zeichnete viel ziere Risse,
behorchte alle Hindernisse,—
dann wurden mir die Pläne krank:
es wirrten sich wie Dorngerank
die Linien und die Ovale,
bis tief in mir mit einem Male
aus einem Griff ins Ungewisse
dir frommste aller Formen sprang.

Ich kann mein Werk nicht überschaun
und fühle doch: es steht vollendet.
Aber, die Augen abgewendet,
will ich es immer wieder baun.

» » »

So ist mein Tagwerk, über dem
mein Schatten liegt wie eine Schale.
Und bin ich auch wie Laub und Lehm,
sooft ich bete oder male
ist Sonntag, und ich bin im Tale
ein jubelndes Jerusalem.

Ich bin die stolze Stadt des Herrn
und sage ihn mit hundert Zungen;
in mir ist Davids Dank verklungen:
ich lag in Harfendämmerungen
und atmete den Abendstern.

in the hour that affirmed me
by one movement of my hand.

I sketched so many subtle lines,
envisioned every obstacle—
but then my plans were undermined:
the lines and ovals twisted into
thorny shrubbery.
Until quite deep inside of me,
while reaching for uncertainty,
the truest form emerged.

I cannot control the art that I do;
still, I feel it stands complete.
And with eyes closed I do intend
to be always creating anew.

》》》

Such is my daily labor over which
lies my shadow like a shell.
And though I am like leaves and loam,
as often as I pray or paint
it's Sunday and deep down I am
joyful Jerusalem.

I am the proud city of the Lord
and I proclaim him with a hundred voices;
in me the praises of David resound.
I lie reclining in the twilight of the harp
while breathing the evening star.

Nach Aufgang gehen meine Gassen.
Und ich bin lang vom Volk verlassen,
so ists: damit ich größer bin.
Ich höre jeden in mir schreiten
und breite meine Einsamkeiten
von Anbeginn zu Anbeginn.

» » »

Ihr vielen unbestürmten Städte,
habt ihr euch nie den Feind ersehnt?
O daß er euch belagert hätte
ein langes schwankendes Jahrzehnt.

Bis ihr ihn trostlos und in Trauern,
bis daß ihr hungernd ihn ertrugt;
er liegt wie Landschaft vor den Mauern,
denn also weiß er auszudauern
um jene, die er heimgesucht.

Schaut aus vom Rande eurer Dächer:
da lagert er und wird nicht matt
und wird nicht weniger und schwächer
und schickt nicht Droher und Versprecher
und Überreder in die Stadt.

Er ist der große Mauerbrecher,
der eine stumme Arbeit hat.

» » »

Ich komme aus meinen Schwingen heim,
mit denen ich mich verlor.

After I rise, my pathways depart.
Abandoned by the people I am.
That way I look greater. Again
I hear them walking inside of me,
and so I spread my lonelinesses
from the beginning to start.

» » »

How many of you, unbesieged cities,
have longed for the enemy?
If only he had held you captive once
for a long, shaky century.

Until you would have learned through the years
to endure the sadness, the hunger, the tears;
like a landscape he lies outside the walls
well equipped to wait for as long as it takes
for the ones he wants.

Look out from the edge of your roofs:
there he is sitting untiringly
and doesn't diminish and doesn't grow weak
and doesn't send those who threaten and promise
and seek to convince and beseech.

He is the greatest toppler of walls
whose power is silent speech.

» » »

I am coming home from flying in circles
in which I was lost in the air.

The Book of the Monkish Life 65

Ich war Gesang, und Gott, der Reim,
rauscht noch in meinem Ohr.

Ich werde wieder still und schlicht,
und meine Stimme steht;
es senkte sich mein Angesicht
zu besserem Gebet.
Den andern war ich wie ein Wind,
da ich sie rüttelnd rief.
Weit war ich, wo die Engel sind,
hoch, wo das Licht in Nichts zerrinnt—
Gott aber dunkel tief.

Die Engel sind das letzte Wehn
an seines Wipfels Saum;
daß sie aus seinen Ästen gehn,
ist ihnen wie ein Traum.
Sie glauben dort dem Lichte mehr
als Gottest schwarzer Kraft,
es flüchtete sich Lucifer
in ihre Nachbarschaft.

Er ist der Fürst im Land des Lichts,
und seine Stirne steht
so steil am großen Glanz des Nichts,
daß er, versengten Angesichts,
nach Finsternissen fleht.
Er ist der helle Gott der Zeit,
zu dem sie laut erwacht,
und weil er oft in Schmerzen schreit
und oft in Schmerzen lacht,

I was the song and God the rhyme
who still resounds in my ear.

I return to being modest and calm,
and my voice stops in its track;
my head bows down again
for a richer prayer yet.
To others I had been like a breeze,
for I sought to shake them awake.
Far away I went to where the angels live,
high above, where light no longer can reach—
God, however, lies deep.

The angels are the remotest breeze
on God's head and hem;
that they issue at all from his branches
they conceive as a dream.
There they place trust more in the light
than in God's blackened force;
even Lucifer sought his refuge
in their neighborhood.

He is the prince in the land of light
with his forehead flat
against the great glory of nothingness,
so that, with sunburned face,
he pleads for the dark.
He is the luminous god of the age,
to which she abruptly awakes,
and because he often cries out in pain
and because he often laughs out loud for pain,

glaubt sie an seine Seligkeit
und hangt an seiner Macht.

Die Zeit ist wie ein welker Rand
an einem Buchenblatt.
Sie ist das glänzende Gewand,
das Gott verworfen hat,
als Er, der immer Tiefe war,
ermüdete des Flugs
und sich verbarg vor jedem Jahr,
bis ihm sein wurzelhaftes Haar
durch alle Dinge wuchs.

» » »

Du wirst nur mit der Tat erfaßt,
mit Händen nur erhellt;
ein jeder Sinn ist nur ein Gast
und sehnt sich aus der Welt.

Ersonnen ist ein jeder Sinn,
man fühlt den feinen Saum darin
und daß ihn einer spann:
Du aber kommst und gibst dich hin
und fällst den Flüchtling an.

Ich will nicht wissen, wo du bist,
sprich mir aus überall.
Dein williger Euangelist
verzeichnet alles und vergißt
zu schauen nach dem Schall.

this age believes in his blessedness
and attaches herself to the same.

The age is like the wilting edge
of a beech-tree leaf.
She is the shimmering dress
that God has cast away
when he, who ever was the deep,
grew tired of flying
and hid out prior to each new year
until his rootlike curly hair
dug deep through it all.

》 》 》

You're captured only through the deed,
in actions you shine forth.
And our senses are but guests,
intent to be let go.

Merely conjured up are perceptions;
one senses their lining is thin,
barely sowed in. But I see
how you arrive, surrender, attack
the one who attempts to flee.

I don't want to know where you reside,
just talk to me from all around.
Your submissive evangelist and scribe
records it all and will put aside
the search for the source of the sound.

Ich geh doch immer auf dich zu
mit meinem ganzen Gehn;
denn wer bin ich und wer bist du,
wenn wir uns nicht verstehn?

» » »

Mein Leben hat das gleiche Kleid und Haar
wie aller alten Zaren Sterbestunde.
Die Macht entfremdete nur meinem Munde,
doch meine Reiche, die ich schweigend runde,
versammeln sich in meinem Hintergrunde
und meine Sinne sind noch Gossudar.

Für sie ist beten immer noch: Erbauen,
aus allen Maßen bauen, daß das Grauen
fast wie die Größe wird und schön,—
und: jedes Hinknien und Vertrauen
(daß es die andern nicht beschauen)
mit vielen goldenen und blauen
und bunten Kuppeln überhöhn.

Denn was sind Kirchen und sind Klöster
in ihrem Steigen und Erstehn
als Harfen, tönende Vertröster,
durch die die Hände Halberlöster
vor Königen und Jungfraun gehn.

» » »

Und Gott befiehlt mir, daß ich schreibe:

I walk forever toward you
with a single mind and strong;
for who would I be and who would you
if we didn't get along?

» » »

My life wears the same old dress and hair
as all the ancient czars while dying.
Except I don't have their might,
and my kingdoms, which I quietly build,
are gathering way back within
the empire of my mind.

To the czars prayer only means:
building to utter extremes,
so terror begins to resemble great beauty and grace—
and: each genuflection and gesture of trust
(to ensure that no one will notice)
is with golden and blue and multicolored
cupolas covered up.

After all, what are churches and convents
in their emerging and rising up:
like harps they spread their comforting strings,
through which run the hands of the semisaved
before statues of saints and kings.

» » »

And then God orders that I write:

Den Königen sei Grausamkeit.
Sie ist der Engel vor der Liebe,
und ohne diesen Bogen bliebe
mir keine Brücke in die Zeit.

Und Gott befiehlt mir, daß ich male:

Die Zeit ist mir mein tiefstes Weh,
so legte ich in ihre Schale:
das wache Weib, die Wundenmale,
den reichen Tod (daß er sie zahle),
der Städte bange Bacchanale,
den Wahnsinn und die Könige.

Und Gott befiehlt mir, daß ich baue:

Denn König bin ich von der Zeit.
Dir aber bin ich nur der graue
Mitwisser deiner Einsamkeit.
Und bin das Auge mit der Braue . . .

Das über meine Schulter schaue
von Ewigkeit zu Ewigkeit.

» » »

Es tauchten tausend Theologen
in deines Namens alte Nacht.
Jungfrauen sind zu dir erwacht,
und Jünglinge in Silber zogen
und schimmerten in dir, du Schlacht.

I've empowered kings to commit cruelty.
It is the angel preceding grace,
and without this landmark I wouldn't have
a bridge into this age.

And then God orders that I paint:

This present age is my deepest woe,
so I painted on its empty face:
the waking woman, the wounds of Christ,
the well-to-do death (so he'll pay for them),
the frantic nightlife of every town,
the kings and the insane.

And then God orders that I build:

For I am the marker of history.
But to you I am only the stony-gray
confidant of your hermit's life.
Beneath the brow I am the eye . . .

which examines my doings from behind
from ever to evermore.

〉〉〉

A thousand theologians dived
into the secrets of your name.
And virgins did awake to you,
and youth set out in silver gear
reflecting you, you fight.

In deinen langen Bogengängen
begegneten die Dichter sich
und waren Könige von Klängen
und mild und tief und meisterlich.

Du bist die sanfte Abendstunde,
die alle Dichter ähnlich macht;
du drängst dich dunkel in die Munde,
und im Gefühl von einem Funde
umgibt ein jeder dich mit Pracht.

Dich heben hunderttausend Harfen
wie Schwingen aus der Schweigsamkeit.
Und deine alten Winde warfen
zu allen Dingen und Bedarfen
den Hauch von deiner Herrlichkeit.

» » »

Die Dichter haben dich verstreut
(es ging ein Sturm durch alles Stammeln),
ich aber will dich wieder sammeln
in dem Gefäß, daß dich erfreut.

Ich wanderte in vielem Winde;
da triebst du tausendmal darin.
Ich bringe alles was ich finde:
als Becher brauchte dich der Blinde,
sehr tief verbarg dich das Gesinde,
der Bettler aber hielt dich hin;
und manchmal war bei einem Kinde
ein großes Stück von deinem Sinn.

In your long archways poets met
and there exchanged the gems they found,
becoming mighty kings of sounds,
mild, deep, and masterful.

You are the gentle evening hour
which makes all poets similar;
you squeeze yourself into their mouths,
and, feeling proud of what they found,
they decorate your brow.

Like wings a hundred thousand harps
raise, out of silence, high your name.
And bygone breezes added to
all objects and necessities
the breath of your acclaim.

» » »

The poets scattered you about
(a storm swept through their stuttering);
but I would like to scoop you up
into a cup you like.

I roamed about in many a wind
in which you twirled a thousandfold.
I'll gather up what I can find—
you quenched the thirsting of the blind,
the common worker muffled you,
the beggar's hand held out your smile;
and sometimes one could find a piece
of you within a child.

Du siehst, daß ich ein Sucher bin.

Einer, der hinter seinen Händen
verborgen geht und wie ein Hirt;
(mögst du den Blick der ihn beirrt,
den Blick der Fremden von ihm wenden).
Einer der träumt, dich zu vollenden
und: daß er sich vollenden wird.

» » »

Selten ist Sonne in Sobór.
Die Wände wachsen aus Gestalten,
und durch die Jungfraun und die Alten
drängt sich, wie Flügel im Entfalten,
das goldene, das Kaiser-Tor.

An seinem Säulenrand verlor
die Wand sich hinter den Ikonen;
und, die im stillen Silber wohnen,
die Steine, steigen wie ein Chor
und fallen wieder in die Kronen
und schweigen schöner als zuvor.

Und über sie, wie Nächte blau,
von Angesichte blaß,
schwebt, die dich freuete, die Frau:
die Pförtnerin, der Morgentau,
die dich umblüht wie eine Au
und ohne Unterlaß.

Die Kuppel ist voll deines Sohns
und bindet rund den Bau.

You see that I still seek.

I'm one who watches secretly,
and works. I am the shepherd type
(o, would you lift the stranger's gaze
that puzzles and confuses me).
I'm one who dreams to make you whole
and be made whole in turn.

» » »

There rarely is sun in Sobor.
Walls emerge out of statues and figures,
and past the women young and aged
looms urgently like fledgling wings
the emperor's golden gate.

Along the edge of its pillars
icons cover up the wall;
and the stones that glisten in silver
rise heavenward like a chorus
and return again to their bases
more magnificent than before.

And above it all, as on navy-blue nights,
hovers the Virgin who delighted you so,
with her face rather white, to be
the guardian angel, the morning dew,
the one who embellishes you like the lea
to no end.

The cupola is full of your Son
and ties together the entire dome.

Willst du geruhen deines Throns,
den ich in Schauern schau.

» » »

Da trat ich als ein Pilger ein
und fühlte voller Qual
an meiner Stirne dich, du Stein.
Mit Lichtern, sieben an der Zahl,
umstellte ich dein dunkles Sein
und sah in jedem Bilde dein
bräunliches Muttermal.

Da stand ich, wo die Bettler stehn,
die schlecht und hager sind:
aus ihrem Auf- und Niederwehn
begriff ich dich, du Wind.
Ich sah den Bauer, überjahrt,
bärtig wie Joachim,
und daraus, wie er dunkel ward,
von lauter Ähnlichen umschart,
empfand ich dich wie nie so zart,
so ohne Wort geoffenbart
in allen und in ihm.

Du läßt der Zeit den Lauf,
und dir ist niemals Ruh darin:
der Bauer findet deinen Sinn
und hebt ihn auf und wirft ihn hin
und hebt ihn wieder auf.

» » »

Will you now descend upon your throne
which I'm beholding with woe?

» » »

So I entered the church in piety
and sensed in painful shock
you, on my forehead, the Rock.
With seven candles I had lit
I enclosed you in your lightless life
and in every icon I discerned
your birthmark dark.

There I stood where the beggars stand
who look so miserable and mangled;
from their steady coming and going
I comprehended you, the Wind.
I saw the farmer advanced in years
bearded like Joachim
and by the way he collected himself,
similar to the others around,
I felt you as I never have,
so mild and without words portrayed
in everything and him.

You grant this age to run its course,
though are never quite at ease with it;
the farmer comes to find your face
and picks it up and throws it down
and picks it up again.

» » »

Wie der Wächter in den Weingeländen
seine Hütte hat und wacht,
bin ich Hütte, Herr, in deinen Händen
und bin Nacht, o Herr, von deiner Nacht.

Weinberg, Weide, alter Apfelgarten,
Acker, der kein Frühjahr überschlägt,
Feigenbaum, der auch im marmorharten
Grunde hundert Früchte trägt:

Duft geht aus aus deinen runden Zweigen.
Und du fragst nicht, ob ich wachsam sei;
furchtlos, aufgelöst in Säften, steigen
deine Tiefen still an mir vorbei.

» » »

Gott spricht zu jedem nur, eh er ihn macht,
dann geht er schweigend mit ihm aus der Nacht.
Aber die Worte, eh jeder beginnt,
diese wolkigen Worte, sind:
Von deinen Sinnen hinausgesandt,
geh bis an deiner Sehnsucht Rand;
gib mir Gewand.

Hinter den Dingen wachse als Brand,
daß ihre Schatten, ausgespannt,
immer mich ganz bedecken.

Laß dir Alles geschehn: Schönheit und Schrecken.
Man muß nur gehn: Kein Gefühl ist das fernste.
Laß dich von mir nicht trennen.

Like the guard who watches and waits
in his hut amidst orchards and yards,
so I am hut, my Lord, within your hands
and night within your dark.

Vineyard, field, meadow, apple yard—
never missing a spring's round;
fig tree I am which even bears fruit
in spite of the rock-hard ground.

Your branches send out their aroma.
You've never asked, did I smell;
and your hidden powers climb past me
distilled, fearless, and tame.

》 》 》

God talks quite audibly before one is created,
then walks in silence beside you into the night.
But the words, before one is given one's start,
these cloudy words are:
Guided by your senses you are sent;
walk to the rim of your desire;
be my attire.

Grow like fire behind the scenes
so your shadows stretch and hover,
becoming my cover.

Allow it all to happen: beauty and terror.
Just press on! No feeling is an error.
But don't get severed from me.

Nah ist das Land,
das sie das Leben nennen.

Du wirst es erkennen
an seinem Ernste.

Gib mir die Hand.

» » »

Ich war bei den ältesten Mönchen, den Malern und
    Mythenmeldern,
die schrieben ruhig Geschichten und zeichneten Runen
    des Ruhms.
Und ich seh dich in meinen Gesichten mit Winden,
    Wassern und Wäldern
rauschend am Rande des Christentums,
du Land, nicht zu lichten.

Ich will dich erzählen, ich will dich beschaun und
    beschreiben,
nicht mit Bol und mit Gold, nur mit Tinte aus
    Apfelbaumrinden;
ich kann auch mit Perlen dich nicht an die Blätter binden,
und das zitterndste Bild, das mir meine Sinne erfinden,
du würdest es blind durch dein einfaches Sein übertreiben.

So will ich die Dinge in dir nur bescheiden und
    schlichthin benamen,
will die Könige nennen, die ältesten, woher sie kamen,
und will ihre Taten und Schlachten berichten am Rand
    meiner Seiten.

Close is this land
which one calls life.

You will recognize it
by its strife.

Take my hand.

» » »

I lived with the oldest monks, the painters, the mongers
      of myths;
they quietly wrote their stories, painting the symbols
      of wealth.
And I see you in many a vision of winds, waters,
      and woods.
On the verge of Christendom you lie and I hear
      your rush,
you land, that no one can grasp.

I want to record you, observe you, describe—
not with cinnabar red and gold, just in ink of the apple
      tree's rind.
Even with beads I cannot tie you to the page,
and the most tottering image my senses contrive,
you blindly outdo by just being alive.

Therefore I wish to be modest and brief in my naming
      of things.
Will report of the kings, the oldest, and whence they came
and note their deeds and battles of ages on my
      pages' rim.

Denn du bist der Boden. Dir sind nur wie Sommer die
     Zeiten,
und du denkst an die nahen nicht anders als an die
     entfernten,
und ob sie dich tiefer besamen und besser bebauen lernten:
du fühlst dich nur leise berührt von den ähnlichen Ernten
und hörst weder Säer noch Schnitter, die über dich
     schreiten.

» » »

Du dunkelnder Grund, geduldig erträgst du die Mauern.
Und vielleicht erlaubst du noch eine Stunde den Städten
     zu dauern
und gewährst noch zwei Stunden den Kirchen und
     einsamen Klöstern
und lässest fünf Stunden noch Mühsal allen Erlöstern
und siehst noch sieben Stunden das Tagwerk des Bauern—:

Eh du wieder Wald wirst und Wasser und wachsende
     Wildnis
          in der Stunde der unerfaßlichen Angst,
          da du dein unvollendetes Bildnis
          von allen Dingen zurückverlangst.

Gib mir noch eine kleine Weile Zeit: ich will die Dinge
     so wie keiner lieben,
          bis sie dir alle würdig sind und weit.
          Ich will nur sieben Tage, sieben
          auf die sich keiner noch geschrieben,
          sieben Seiten Einsamkeit.

For you are the ground. To you summer is
     every day,
and you view those close by the same as those away;
and whether they sow in you deeper or plow better the
     ground:
You are only slightly astounded by their similar yield.
And you hear neither sower nor cutter who walk over
     you—the field.

» » »

You darkening ground, with patience you bear the walls.
And perhaps you grant for an hour the cities to last,
and grant yet two hours the monasteries and churches,
and give yet five hours of misery to the redeemed,
and look upon the farmer's work for seven hours yet—

Before you become again forest and water and wilderness
     growth
          in the hour of incomprehensible terror and death,
          where you demand from it all
          your incomplete image back.

Just give me time and I'll love the things as no one
     ever did,
          until they all have become wide and worthy of you.
          I only need seven days, I guess,
          which no one has claimed or covered before,
          seven pages of loneliness.

Wem du das Buch gibst, welches die umfaßt,
der wird gebückt über den Blättern bleiben.
Es sei denn, daß du ihn in Händen hast,
um selbst zu schreiben.

》》》

So bin ich nur als Kind erwacht,
so sicher im Vertraun
nach jeder Angst und jeder Nacht
dich wieder anzuschaun.
Ich weiß, sooft mein Denken mißt,
wie tief, wie lang, wie weit—:
du aber bist und bist und bist,
umzittert von der Zeit.

Mir ist, als wär ich jetzt zugleich
Kind, Knab und Mann und mehr.
Ich fühle: nur der Ring ist reich
durch seine Wiederkehr.

Ich danke dir, du tiefe Kraft,
die immer leiser mit mir schafft
wie hinter vielen Wänden;
jetzt ward mir erst der Werktag schlicht
und wie ein heiliges Gesicht
zu meinen dunklen Händen.

》》》

Daß ich nicht war vor einer Weile,
weißt du davon? Und du sagst nein.

Whoever you give this book I will write
will keep on reading with downward gaze.
Unless, of course, you are holding his hand
and he in turn becomes scribe.

》 》 》

I tend to wake up like a child
so certain in my trust:
after every night and every worry,
I look at you at last.
I know as often as I measure my thoughts,
how deep, how long, how wide:
but you are is, and was, and will,
and quiver within time.

It seems as if I were at once
child, boy, and man, and more.
I know the cycle is only complete
as each element returns.

I give you thanks, you mighty force,
which ever gentler works on me
in quiet and behind closed doors;
so working days are pure again
and contrast with my unclean hands
like holy imagery.

》 》 》

Do you realize that a few years ago
I didn't exist? But you say, No.

Da fühl ich, wenn ich nur nicht eile,
so kann ich nie vergangen sein.

Ich bin ja mehr als Traum im Traume.
Nur was sich sehnt nach einem Saume,
ist wie ein Tag und wie ein Ton;
es drängt sich fremd durch deine Hände,
daß es die viele Freiheit fände,
und traurig lassen sie davon.

So blieb das Dunkel dir allein,
und, wachsend in die leere Lichte,
erhob sich eine Weltgeschichte
aus immer blinderem Gestein.
Ist einer noch, der daran baut?
Die Massen wollen wieder Massen,
die Steine sind wie losgelassen

und keiner ist von dir behauen.

》 》 》

Es lärmt das Licht im Wipfel deines Baumes
und macht dir all Dinge bunt und eitel,
sie finden dich erst wenn der Tag verglomm.
Die Dämmerung, die Zärtlichkeit des Raumes,
legt tausend Hände über tausend Scheitel,
und unter ihnen wird das Fremde fromm.

Du willst die Welt nicht anders an dich halten
als so, mit dieser sanftesten Gebärde.
Aus ihren Himmeln greifst du dir die Erde
und fühlst sie unter deines Mantels Falten.

So perhaps if I didn't hurry so much,
I could keep on going for good.

Am I not more than a dream within fog?
Only that which longs for limits
makes up a day and creates a note;
it awkwardly pushes through your hands,
seeking to escape from you,
so your hands sadly let go.

Darkness was all that was left to you,
so into the empty clearing grew
the history of the world.
It emerged from ever more stupid stone.
I wonder, Are they still building on it?
Masses desire ever more mass,
stones are left to fall as they do,

yet none has been hewn by you.

» » »

The light is making noises in your treetops,
inciting things to be frivolous and bright
so they can find you only when the night arrives.
The darkling dusk, the soft caress of space,
extends its many hands to many heads,
and by their touch the quaint and crude turn mild.

You want to hug the world no differently
than only with the gentlest of holds.
You pluck the earth out of a sea of sky
and feel it prod you now beneath your robe.

Du hast so eine leise Art zu sein.
Und jene, die dir laute Namen weihn,
sind schon vergessen deiner Nachbarschaft.

Von deinen Händen, die sich bergig heben,
steigt, unsern Sinnen das Gesetz zu geben,
mit dunkler Stirne deine stumme Kraft.

» » »

Du Williger, und deine Gnade kam
immer in alle ältesten Gebärden.
Wenn einer die Hände zusammenflicht,
so daß sie zahm
und um ein kleines Dunkel sind—:
auf einmal fühlt er dich in ihnen werden,
und wie im Winde
senkt sich sein Gesicht
in Scham.

Und da versucht er, auf dem Stein zu liegen
und aufzustehn, wie er bei andern sieht,
und seine Mühe ist, dich einzuwiegen,
aus Angst, daß er dein Wachsein schon verriet.

Denn wer dich fühlt, kann sich mit dir nicht brüsten;
er ist erschrocken, bang um dich und flieht
vor allen Fremden, die dich merken müßten:

Du bist das Wunder in den Wüsten,
das Ausgewanderten geschieht.

» » »

You surely have a silent way of being yourself.
And those who baptize you with blaring names
are far removed from your side.

From your hands, cupped into mountains, climbs
with darkened brow your quiet force
and gives us your commands and laws.

» » »

You willing one, your mercy came
forever in familiar moves.
Whenever someone folds his hands
so they are calmed and lying tame
around a speck of dark—
and when he feels you grow in them,
just as the gentle breezes blow,
he drops his head in shame.

And then he keeps flat to the floor
and scrambles back, like others do,
and tries to cradle you and fears
he'd shown you were awake.

Whoever sees you cannot boast of it;
he is confused, afraid for you, and flees
from strangers, who should know you're here—

You miracle in desert sand
that only exiles see.

» » »

Eine Stunde vom Rande des Tages,
und das Land ist zu allem bereit.
Was du sehnst, meine Seele, sag es:

Sei Heide und, Heide, sei weit.
Habe alte, alte Kurgane,
wachsend und kaumerkannt,
wenn es Mond wird über das plane
langvergangene Land.
Gestalte dich, Stille. Gestalte
die Dinge (es ist ihre Kindheit,
sie werden dir willig sein).
Sei Heide, sei Heide, sei Heide,
dann kommt vielleicht auch der Alte,
den ich kaum von der Nacht unterscheide,
und bringt seine riesige Blindheit
in mein horchendes Haus herein.

Ich seh ihn sitzen und sinnen,
nicht über mich hinaus;
für ihn ist alles innen,
Himmel und Heide und Haus.
Nur die Lieder sind ihm verloren,
die er nie mehr beginnt;
aus vielen tausend Ohren
trank sie die Zeit und der Wind;
aus den Ohren der Toren.

» » »

Und dennoch: mir geschieht,
als ob ich ein jedes Lied
tief in mir ihm ersparte.

Just one hour at the end of the day
and the landscape lies fully prepared.
What you long for, my soul, now say:

Be heather and heath, spreading far.
Have old and ancient burial mounds,
hardly known, abound—
just as soon as the moon comes out
over the long-lost land.
Create yourself, Silence. Create
all things (being young,
they are easily plied).
Be moor, be heath, be plain,
so the Ancient One may arrive,
the one I can hardly discern at night,
and be carrying his monumental blindness
into my harkening home.

I see him sit and ponder,
but never beyond my reach;
to him all life resides within,
heaven, home, and heath.
Only his songs he has lost,
so these he never recites;
for from the many ears of the past
the wind drank them up by the gates.

» » »

And still I believe
I might capture each song
deep within me,

Er schweigt hinterm bebenden Barte,
er möchte sich wiedergewinnen
aus seinen Melodien.
Da komm ich zu seinen Knien:

und seine Lieder rinnen
rauschend zurück in ihn.

While he is quiet, beard aquiver,
bent to find in his melodies
himself.
Then I support his knees:

and his songs surge back
to be his.

» » » Das Buch von der Pilgerschaft

Dich wundert nicht des Sturmes Wucht,—
du hast ihn wachsen sehn;—
die Bäume flüchten. Ihre Flucht
schafft schreitende Alleen.
Da weißt du, der von dem sie fliehn
ist der, zu dem du gehst,
und deine Sinne singen ihn,
wenn du am Fenster stehst.

Des Sommers Wochen standen still,
es stieg der Bäume Blut;
jetzt fühlst du, daß es fallen will
in den der Alles tut.
Du glaubtest schon erkannt die Kraft,
als du die Frucht erfaßt,
jetzt wird sie wieder rätselhaft,
und du bist wieder Gast.

Der Sommer war so wie dein Haus,
drin weißt du alles stehn—
jetzt mußt du in dein Herz hinaus
wie in die Ebene gehn.
Die große Einsamkeit beginnt,
die Tage werden taub,
aus deinen Sinne nimmt der Wind
die Welt wie welkes Laub.

» » » The Book of Pilgrimage

You, Pilgrim, are used to hurricanes;
after all, you have seen them brew;
the treetops flee and their escape
makes pathways in the woods.
And then you know the one they flee
is he to whom you pray,
and all your senses sing his songs
while peering through the pane.

Summer seemed perpetual,
the sap of the trees rose high;
and now you feel it wants to fall
into him who made this life.
You thought you could conclude your quest
once you had reaped the fruit,
but now the fruit turns wondrous
and you again are guest.

The summer was like a resort—
you knew your way around.
But then you needed to return
to the desert of your heart.
The lengthy solitude begins,
the days turn dull again;
the wind removes, like wilted leaves,
the world you once could name.

Durch ihre leeren Zweige sieht
der Himmel, den du hast;
sei Erde jetzt und Abendlied
und Land, darauf er paßt.
Demütig sei jetzt wie ein Ding,
zu Wirklichkeit gereift,—
daß Der, von dem die Kunde ging,
dich fühlt, wenn er dich greift.

» » »

Ich bete wieder, du Erlauchter,
du hörst mich wieder durch den Wind,
weil meine Tiefen niegebrauchter
rauschender Worte mächtig sind.

Ich war zerstreut; an Widersacher
in Stücken war verteilt mein Ich.
O Gott, mich lachten alle Lacher
und alle Trinker tranken mich.

In Höfen hab ich mich gesammelt
aus Abfall und aus altem Glas,
mit halbem Mund dich angestammelt,
dich, Ewiger aus Ebenmaß.
Wie hob ich meine halben Hände
zu dir in namelosem Flehn
daß ich die Augen wiederfände,
mit denen ich dich angesehn.

Ich war ein Haus nach einem Brand,
darin nur Mörder manchmal schlafen,

Through branches bare the sky looks down,
the only sky you have;
be ground now, evening song and land,
with which this sky can blend.
Be subject like a tool for use,
mature and fit for much—
so he, of whom we often heard,
will know you at his touch.

» » »

I am praying again, you blessed one;
you can hear what I say in the wind;
for my soul is enabled to capture again
brand-new words that arise from within.

I was disjointed; piecemeal my soul
was doled out to opponent and foe.
God, I was the laugh of every mouth
and the drink that poured forth from each cup.

In back alleys I did meditate,
near garbage and broken glass;
with limpid lips I stammered at you,
you the harmonious one.
How did I lift my half-formed hands
to you in nameless pleas,
petitioning to find again
a way to see your face!

I was the house wrecked by a blaze,
in which one sees now felons sleep

eh ihre hungerigen Strafen
sie weiterjagen in das Land;
ich war wie eine Stadt am Meer,
wenn eine Seuche sie bedrängte,
die sich wie eine Leiche schwer
den Kindern an die Hände hängte.

Ich war mir fremd wie irgendwer,
und wußte nur von ihm, daß er
einst meine junge Mutter kränkte
als sie mich trug,
und daß ihr Herz, das eingeengte,
sehr schmerzhaft an mein Keimen schlug.

Jezt bin ich wieder aufgebaut
aus allen Stücken meiner Schande,
und sehne mich nach einem Bande,
nach einem einigen Verstande,
der mich wie ein Ding überschaut,—
nach deines Herzens großen Händen—
(o kämen sie doch auf mich zu).
Ich zähle mich, mein Gott, und du,
du hast das Recht, mich zu verschwenden.

» » »

Ich bin derselbe noch, der kniete
vor dir in mönchischem Gewand:
der tiefe, dienende Levite,
den du erfüllt, der dich erfand.
Die Stimme einer stillen Zelle,
an der die Welt vorüberweht,—

before their haunting sentences
chase them out in the day.
I was the city by the sea
overcome by pestilence
which, like a corpse, weighed heavily
and clung to children's hands.

I was a stranger to myself
and only knew with certainty
that I had hurt my mother's womb
these months she carried me,
and that her heart, severely cramped,
struck painfully at me.

But I gained back my strength,
recovered from these shreds of shame
and seek this greatest cord that binds—
a mutual thought, a fitting mind,
which views me as a whole;
I long for your receiving hands
(if only they would reach for me).
We make a team, with you in charge
of using me for thee.

))))))

I'm still the same who often knelt
before you in his monkish cloak;
the serious Levite serving you,
whom you made glad, who sought you out.
I am the sound inside my cell,
the room the world keeps rushing past;

und du bist immer noch die Welle,
die über alle Dinge geht.

Es *ist* nichts andres. Nur ein Meer,
aus dem die Länder manchmal steigen.
Es *ist* nichts andres denn ein Schweigen
von schönen Engeln und von Geigen,
und der Verschwiegene ist der,
zu dem sich all Dinge neigen,
von seiner Stärke Strahlen schwer.

Bist du denn Alles,—ich der Eine,
der sich ergibt und sich empört?
Bin ich denn nicht das Allgemeine,
bin ich nicht *Alles*, wenn ich weine,
und du der Eine, der es hört?

Hörst du denn etwas neben mir?
Sind da noch Stimmen außer meiner?
Ist da ein Sturm? Auch ich bin einer,
und meine Wälder winken dir.

Ist da ein Lied, ein krankes, kleines,
das dich am Micherhören stört,—
auch ich bin eines, höre meines,
das einsam ist und unerhört.

Ich bin derselbe noch, der bange
dich manchmal fragte, wer du seist.
Nach jedem Sonnenuntergange
bin ich verwundet und verwaist,
ein blasser Allem Abgelöster

and you are still the wafting wave
who hovers over all.

It's nothing but a vast sea
out of which the nations climb.
It's nothing but the quiet
out of which angels and violins chime,
and the silent one is he
to whom all things give praise
imbued with his powers' rays.

Are you it all, and I just part
who yields, gives in, and is distraught?
Am I not even "on the whole,"
am I not *all* when I shed tears
and you the part that hears?

Did you hear anything else but me?
Are there other voices besides my own?
Is there a storm? I am one too
with trees that wave at you.

Is there a song, a sickly and small one
that keeps you from answering me—
I hold a song too, please listen to mine,
which is lonely and unlistened to.

I am still the same, the fearful one
who sometimes asked you who you were.
The one who hurts when dusk arrives,
a pale one severed from his life,
an orphaned outcast to the crowd,

und ein Verschmähter jeder Schar,
und alle Dinge stehn wie Klöster,
in denen ich gefangen war.
Dann brauch ich dich, du Eingeweihter,
du sanfter Nachbar jeder Not,
du meines Leidens leiser Zweiter,
du Gott, dann brauch ich dich wie Brot.
Du weißt vielleicht nicht, wie die Nächte
für Menschen, die nicht schlafen, sind:
da sind sie alle Ungerechte,
der Greis, die Jungfrau und das Kind.
Sie fahren auf wie totgesagt,
von schwarzen Dingen nah umgeben,
und ihre weißen Hände beben,
verwoben in ein wildes Leben
wie Hunde in ein Bild der Jagd.
Vergangenes steht noch bevor,
und in der Zukunft liegen Leichen,
ein Mann im Mantel pocht am Tor,
und mit dem Auge und dem Ohr
ist noch kein erstes Morgenzeichen,
kein Hahnruf ist noch zu erreichen.
Die Nacht ist wie ein großes Haus.
Und mit der Angst der wunden Hände
reißen sie Türen in die Wände,—
dann kommen Gänge ohne Ende,
und nirgends ist ein Tor hinaus.

Und so, mein Gott, ist *jede* Nacht;
immer sind welche aufgewacht,
die gehn und gehn und dich nicht finden.
Hörst du sie mit dem Schritt von Blinden

to whom all things that locked me in
like monasteries seem.
That's when I need you, Confidant,
you neighbor in each need,
you partner in my suffering—
I need you then like bread.
You probably don't know how those nights are
to people whom sleep escapes:
They all feel like sinners and outlaws,
the old man, the child, the maid.
On a stretcher they are carried like dead
surrounded by objects in black;
their limpid hands tremble entwined
into chases after life that thrives,
like dogs in a painted hunting scene.
The past has yet to be relived,
the future's paved with corpse and death;
a man in cloak knocks on the gate,
and neither eye nor ear can spy
a sign of morning's wake;
no rooster's crow appears.
The night is like a giant house.
And terror causes mangled hands
to tear up walls for doors—
then hallways spring up everywhere—
with exits nowhere near.

Such, Lord, is *every* night I have;
where people appear who are waking up,
who sought you in a fruitless walk.
Can you discern the gait with which

das Dunkel treten?
Auf Treppen, die sich niederwinden,
hörst du sie beten?
Hörst du sie fallen auf den schwarzen Steinen?
Du mußt sie weinen hören; denn sie weinen.

Ich suche dich, weil sie vorübergehn
an meiner Tür. Ich kann sie beinah sehn.
Wen soll ich rufen, wenn nicht *den*,
der dunkel ist und nächtiger als Nacht.
Den Einzigen, der ohne Lampe wacht
und doch nicht bangt; den Tiefen, den das Licht
noch nicht verwöhnt hat und von dem ich weiß,
weil er mit Bäumen aus der Erde bricht
und weil er leis
als Duft in mein gesenktes Angesicht
aus Erde steigt.

» » »

Du Ewiger, du hast dich mir gezeigt.
Ich liebe dich wie einen lieben Sohn,
der mich einmal verlassen hat als Kind,
weil ihn das Schicksal rief auf einen Thron,
vor dem die Länder alle Täler sind.
Ich bin zurückgeblieben wie ein Greis,
der seinen großen Sohn nichtmehr versteht
und wenig von den neuen Dingen weiß,
zu welchen seines Samens Wille geht.
Ich bebe manchmal für dein tiefes Glück,
das auf so vielen fremden Schiffen fährt,
ich wünsche manchmal dich in mich zurück,

these blind trip in the dark?
On stairways that wind downward
can you perceive them pray?
Do you hear them prostrate on stone?
You must hear them, for they cry.

I am looking for you as they are passing
my door. I can make them out almost.
Who else should I call but the one
who is dark and blacker than the night.
The only one who can watch without lamp
free from fear; the deep, whom the light
did not spoil and whom I've known—
because he erupts from the ground as trees
and because he coils
as fragrance into my lowered face
from soil.

» » »

You, eternal one, did show yourself to me.
I hold you dear as if a son,
who left me while a child,
for fate had called you to a throne
that overlooked the vales.
And I, a hoary man, remained
confused about his grown-up son,
untrained in all the modern things
to which the son is drawn.
I tremble for your perfect bliss
that sails aboard such foreign ships;
at times I wish you back with me

in dieses Dunkel, das dich großgenährt.
Ich bange machmal, daß du nichtmehr bist,
wenn ich mich sehr verliere an die Zeit.
Dann les ich von dir: der Euangelist
schreibt überall von deiner Ewigkeit.

Ich bin der Vater; doch der Sohn ist mehr,
ist alles, was der Vater war, und der,
der er nicht wurde, wird in jenem groß;
er ist die Zukunft und die Wiederkehr,
er ist der Schooß, er ist das Meer. . . .

» » »

Dir ist mein Beten keine Blasphemie:
als schlüge ich in alten Büchern nach,
daß ich dir sehr verwandt bin—tausendfach.

Ich will dir Liebe geben. Die und die. . . .

Liebt man denn einen Vater? Geht man nicht,
wie du von mir gingst, Härte im Gesicht,
von seinen hülflos leeren Händen fort?
Legt man nicht leise sein verwelktes Wort
in alte Bücher, die man selten liest?
Fließt man nicht wie von einer Wasserscheide
von seinem Herzen ab zu Lust und Leide?
Ist uns der Vater denn nicht das, was *war;*
vergangne Jahre, welche fremd gedacht,
veraltete Gebärde, tote Tracht,
verblühte Hände und verblichnes Haar?
Und war er selbst für seine Zeit ein Held,
er ist das Blatt, das wenn wir wachsen, fällt.

inside this womb that brought you up.
And when I'm lost in nagging thought
and worry that you might be dead,
I read of you: The evangelist
writes across his page, You are.

I am the father but the son is more,
is everything the father was; and what
he couldn't be, the son becomes as well;
the son is both the future and the past:
source of rivulets and sea to which they turn.

» » »

My prayers are to you no blasphemy:
for as if I were doing genealogy,
I presume myself a relative of yours—

A thousandfold. I want to give you love.

Does one love a father? Or does one leave,
as you did me, resolve on one's face,
his helplessly empty hands?
Does one not place his wilting words
quietly into never read books?
Does one not, as if from a watershed,
run off his heart to the right and left?
Is the father not a symbol of the past:
of years gone by, appearing strange,
outdated ways, and ancient dress,
of wilted hands and faded hair?
And though acclaimed as hero in his time,
he is the leaf that drops as we progress.

Und sein Sorgfalt ist uns wie ein Alb,
und seine Stimme ist uns wie ein Stein,—
wir möchten seiner Rede hörig sein,
aber wir hören seine Worte halb.
Das große Drama zwischen ihm und uns
lärmt viel zu laut, einander zu verstehn,
wir sehen nur die Formen seines Munds,
aus denen Silben fallen, die vergehn.
So sind wir noch viel ferner ihm als fern,
wenn auch die Liebe uns noch weit verwebt,
erst wenn er sterben muß auf diesem Stern,
sehn wir, daß er auf diesem Stern gelebt.

Das ist der Vater uns. Und ich—ich soll
dich Vater nennen?
Das hieße tausendmal mich von dir trennen.
Du bist mein Sohn. Ich werde dich erkennen,
wie man sein einzigliebes Kind erkennt, auch dann,
wenn es ein Mann geworden ist, ein alter Mann.

» » »

Lösch mir die Augen aus: ich kann dich sehn,
wirf mir die Ohren zu: ich kann dich hören,
und ohne Füße kann ich zu dir gehn,
und ohne Mund noch kann ich dich beschwören.
Brich mir die Arme ab, ich fasse dich
mit meinem Herzen wie mit einer Hand,
halt mir das Herz zu, und mein Hirn wird schlagen,
und wirfst du in mein Hirn den Brand,
so werd ich dich auf meinem Blute tragen.

And his meticulous ways are a nightmare to us,
and his voice grates like a millstone on our nerves—
we desire to pay attention to what he says,
but listen to barely half of his words.
The interplay between him and us
creates a chasm that bars accord;
we only note the outlines of his mouth,
from which drip syllables that pass.
And we grow farther yet apart,
despite the love that ever wraps around;
and only at his death on planet Earth
do we admit he too did live.

So that's a father. And one expects I will
call you my father still?
That would mean a thousandfold
that I had distanced myself from you.
You are my son, my only-loved child,
though the boy is grown up now—and old.

» » »

Extinguish my sight, and I can still see you;
plug up my ears, and I can still hear;
even without feet I can walk toward you,
and without mouth I can still implore.
Break off my arms, and I will hold you
with my heart as if it were a hand;
strangle my heart, and my brain will still throb;
and should you set fire to my brain,
I still can carry you with my blood.

» » »

Und meine Seele ist ein Weib vor dir.
Und ist wie der Naemi Schnur, wie Ruth.
Sie geht bei Tag um deiner Garben Hauf
wie eine Magd, die tiefe Dienste tut.
Aber am Abend steigt sie in die Flut
und badet sich und kleidet sich sehr gut
und kommt zu dir, wenn alles um dich ruht,
und kommt und deckt zu deinen Füßen auf.
Und fragst du sie um Mitternacht, sie sagt
mit tiefer Einfalt: Ich bin Ruth, die Magd.
Spann deine Flügel über deine Magd.
      Du bist der Erbe. . . .

Und meine Seele schläft dann bis es tagt
bei deinen Füßen, warm von deinem Blut.
Und ist ein Weib vor dir. Und ist wie Ruth.

» » »

Du bist der Erbe.
Söhne sind die Erben,
denn Väter sterben.
Söhne stehn und blühn.
      Du bist der Erbe.

» » »

Und du erbst das Grün
vergangner Gärten und das stille Blau
zerfallner Himmel.

» » »

And my soul is like a woman to you.
She is Naomi's band that ties to Ruth.
By day, my soul stacks sheaves of wheat
like a maidservant doing lowly tasks.
But at night, she takes a thorough bath,
perfumes, and dresses very well;
then goes to you when all's asleep,
and turns back the cover by your feet.
And when you wake and ask her to explain,
she naively says: I'm Ruth, the maid.
Spread your cloak over your servant,
you are heir and next of kin. . . .

And then my soul sleeps until dawn
down by your feet, warmed by this blood of yours,
and is your woman—just like Ruth.

» » »

You are the heir.
Sons are the heirs because
fathers will die.
Sons, however, rise and grow.
        You are the heir.

» » »

And you inherit what grew
in gardens long gone and the blue
of a shattered sky.

Tau aus tausend Tagen,
die vielen Sommer, die die Sonnen sagen
und lauter Frühlinge mit Glanz und Klagen
wie viele Briefe einer jungen Frau.
Du erbst die Herbste, die wie Prunkgewänder
in der Erinnerung von Dichtern liegen,
und alle Winter, wie verwaiste Länder,
scheinen sich leise an dich anzuschmiegen.
Du erbst Venedig und Kasan und Rom,
Florenz wird dein sein, der Pisaner Dom,
die Troitzka Lawra und das Monastir,
das unter Kiews Gärten ein Gewirr
von Gängen bildet, dunkel und verschlungen,—
Moskau mit Glocken wie Erinnerungen,—
und Klang wird dein sein: Geigen, Hörner, Zungen,
und jedes Lied, das tief genug erklungen,
wird an dir glänzen wie ein Edelstein.

Für dich nur schließen sich die Dichter ein
und sammeln Bilder, rauschende und reiche,
und gehn hinaus und reifen durch Vergleiche
und sind ihr ganzes Leben so allein. . . .
Und Maler malen ihre Bilder nur,
damit du *unvergänglich* die Natur,
die du vergänglich schufst, zurückempfängst:
alles wird ewig. Sieh, das Weib ist längst
in der Madonna Lisa reif wie Wein;
es müßte nie ein Weib mehr sein,
denn Neues bringt kein neues Weib hinzu.
Die, welche bilden, sind wie du.
Sie wollen Ewigkeit. Sie sagen: Stein,
sei ewig. Und das heißt: sei dein!

You inherit dew from a thousand days,
the many summers declared by the sun,
and the many springs with bliss and pain
like in the many letters of a woman young.
You inherit the falls' royal robes that lie
in the back of poets' minds;
and all the winters, like orphaned lands,
that seem to sidle up to you in quiet.
You inherit Venice and Kasan and Rome,
Florence will be yours, and Pisa's dome;
the Troiska Lavra and that of Pechersk,
which forms a darkened tunnel's maze
below the gardens of Kiev.
You inherit Moscow and her bells and memories—
and sound will be yours: violins, horns, and tongues;
and every song that is resounding deep enough
will decorate you like a precious stone.

For you alone the poets lock their doors
and gather pictures, rife and rich; emerge
much more matured by reams of metaphor,
and still remain alone.
And painters only paint so you'll receive
all nature, which you made to pass,
in paintings that will last;
everything becomes eternal. See,
the Mona Lisa is as ripe as wine;
one wouldn't need another woman ever
for none could add another line.
Those in the art of creating are like you.
They want eternity and say: Stone, you must endure!
And that means: Be God's, be yours!

Und auch, die lieben, sammeln für dich ein:
Sie sind die Dichter einer kurzen Stunde,
sie küssen einem ausdruckslosen Munde
ein Lächeln auf, als formten sie ihn schöner,
und bringen Lust und sind die Angewöhner
zu Schmerzen, welche erst erwachsen machen.
Sie bringen Leiden mit in ihrem Lachen,
Sehnsüchte, welche schlafen, und erwachen,
um aufzuweinen in der fremden Brust.
Sie häufen Rätselhaftes an und sterben,
wie Tiere sterben, ohne zu begreifen,—
aber sie werden vielleicht Enkel haben,
in denen ihre grünen Leben reifen;
durch diese wirst du jene Liebe erben,
die sie sich blind und wie im Schlafe gaben.

So fließt der Dinge Überfluß dir zu.
Und wie die obern Becken von Fontänen
beständig überströmen, wie von Strähnen
gelösten Haares, in die tiefste Schale,—
so fällt die Fülle dir in deine Tale,
wenn Dinge und Gedanken übergehn.

» » »

Ich bin nur einer deiner Ganzgeringen,
der in das Leben aus der Zelle sieht
und der, den Menschen ferner als den Dingen,
nicht wagt zu wägen, was geschieht.
Doch willst du mich vor deinem Angesicht,
aus dem sich dunkel deine Augen heben,
dann halte es für meine Hoffahrt nicht,

And even those in love collect for you:
They are the poets for the shorter run;
they press upon a mouth that has no charm
a smile, as if they molded it anew,
and add their joys and pave the way
for pain, which pushes one to grow.
For they cause love pangs with their jest,
nostalgic moments, which will come and go,
and move to tears the burning breast.
They pile up mysteries, and then they are no more,
like animals, who never ponder or perceive;
perhaps though they left behind grandchildren
in whom their own unripened life will live;
and through their kin you will inherit
the love of those who gave themselves before.

And so abundance is of benefit to you.
And like the upper basins of a fountain
that are forever overflowing as
with strands of hair, unto the deepest pan—
so falls, when thing and thought abound,
the fullness of all things into your hands.

» » »

I am one of your lowliest,
who looks upon life from his cell,
one farther removed from people than things
who dares not speculate on your will.
But if you want me to come before you,
before the dark of your eyes,
I hope you won't think me arrogant

wenn ich dir sage: keiner lebt sein Leben.
Zufälle sind die Menschen, Stimmen, Stücke,
Alltage, Ängste, viele kleine Glücke,
verkleidet schon als Kinder, eingemummt,
als Masken mündig, als Gesicht—verstummt.

Ich denke oft: Schatzhäuser müssen sein,
wo alle diese vielen Leben liegen
wie Panzer oder Sänften oder Wiegen,
in welche nie ein Wirklicher gestiegen,
und wie Gewänder, welche ganz allein
nicht stehen können und sich sinkend schmiegen
an starke Wände aus gewölbtem Stein.

Und wenn ich abends immer weiterginge
aus meinem Garten, drin ich müde bin,—
ich weiß: dann führen alle Wege hin
zum Arsenal der ungelebten Dinge.
Dort ist kein Baum, als legte sich das Land,
und wie um ein Gefängnis hängt die Wand
ganz fensterlos in siebenfachem Ringe.
Und ihre Tore mit den Eisenspangen,
die denen wehren, welche hinverlangen,
und ihre Gitter sind von Menschenhand.

》 》 》

Und doch, obwohl ein jeder von sich strebt
wie aus dem Kerker, der ihn haßt und hält,—
es ist ein großes Wunder in der Welt:
ich fühle: *alles Leben wird gelebt.*

when I say, No one is really alive.
People are just accidents, pieces with voice,
they have common sensations with fears and joys;
as children already they are heavily costumed,
as masks they are vocal, but as faces they are mute.

I often think we would need treasuries
where all these many lives could lie
like suits of armor, cradles, or sedans
into which no real people ever climbed;
or like clothes, which on their own
cannot stand up, hence drape against
the firm, round walls of stone.

And when at dusk I would proceed,
somewhat tired, beyond my yard,
I were to see that all paths lead
to the great arsenal of unlived things.
There is no tree, the land is flat;
like a prison are the walls suspended
without windows seven times around.
And its gates bear iron bands,
and it is fenced off by human hands
to keep those out who want to enter.

» » »

And yet, though everybody seeks to get away
from self as from a cell that hates and keeps
its prisoner in, the greatest miracle is
knowing that still *all life is lived.*

Wer lebt es denn? Sind das die Dinge, die
wie eine ungespielte Melodie
im Abend wie in einer Harfe stehn?
Sind das die Winde, die von Wassern wehn,
sind das die Zweige, die sich Zeichen geben,
sind das die Blumen, die die Düfte weben,
sind das die langen alternden Alleen?
Sind das die warmen Tiere, welche gehn,
sind das die Vögel, die sich fremd erheben?

Wer lebt es denn? Lebst du es, Gott,—das Leben?

» » »

Du bist der Alte, dem die Haare
von Ruß versengt sind und verbrannt,
du bist der große Unscheinbare,
mit deinem Hammer in der Hand.
Du bist der Schmied, das Lied der Jahre,
der immer an dem Amboß stand.

Du bist, der niemals Sonntag hat,
der in die Arbeit Eingekehrte,
der sterben könnte überm Schwerte,
das noch nicht glänzend wird und glatt.
Wenn bei uns Mühle steht und Säge
und alle trunken sind und träge,
dann hört man deine Hammerschläge
an allen Glocken in der Stadt.

Du bist der Mündige, der Meister,
und keiner hat dich lernen sehn;

But who does live it? Is it things
which, like an unplayed melody,
hang about a harp at night?
Is it the winds that come from the sea,
is it the branches that give each other signs,
is it the flowers that release their scent,
is it the long and ancient alleys?
Is it the warm-blooded animals that walk,
is it the birds that rise up from valleys?

Who lives life really? Is it you, God?

» » »

You are the Ancient One, whose hair
is marred by soot and singed by flame;
you are the utmost indistinct;
and with a hammer in your hand,
you are the blacksmith, song of years,
who by his anvil stands.

You are the one without a break
who ever finds himself at work,
who slaves away over a sword
that still remains uncouth, unsmooth.
When our mills and saws have stopped
and people are asleep or slouch,
then one can hear your hammer drone
in every bell of town.

You are the grown-up and the master,
and no one ever saw you train;

ein Unbekannter, Hergereister,
von dem bald flüsternder, bald dreister
die Reden und Gerüchte gehn.

》 》 》

Gerüchte gehn, die dich vermuten,
und Zweifel gehn, die dich verwischen.
Die Trägen und die Träumerischen
mißtrauen ihren eignen Gluten
und wollen, daß die Berge bluten,
denn eher glauben sie dich nicht.

Du aber senkst dein Angesicht.

Du könntest den Bergen die Adern aufschneiden
als Zeichen eines großen Gerichts;
aber dir liegt nichts
an den Heiden.

Du willst nicht streiten mit allen Listen
und nicht suchen die Liebe des Lichts;
denn dir liegt nichts
an den Christen.

Dir liegt an den Fragenden nichts.
Sanften Gesichts
siehst du den Tragenden zu.

》 》 》

a stranger, one from out of town
of whom in whispers or out loud
wild rumors mill about.

» » »

Some rumors run suspecting you,
some doubts emerge that wipe you out.
The slow at heart, the dream-enthralled
distrust their spontaneity;
they want to see the mountains bleed
or else they won't believe.

But you only lower your face.

You could, if you wished, cut open the veins
of the mountains as a sign of your court;
but with pagans
you deal not.

You don't like to argue with strategy,
nor seek to instill the love of light;
for you'd rather not fight
for Christians.

The questioner you'd rather not bother.
But you gently look upon
all who labor on.

» » »

Alle, welche dich suchen, versuchen dich.
Und die, so dich finden, binden dich
an Bild und Gebärde.

Ich aber will dich begreifen
wie dich die Erde begreift;
mit meinem Reifen
reift
dein Reich.

Ich will von dir keine Eitelkeit,
die dich beweist.
Ich weiß, daß die Zeit
anders heißt als du.

Tu mir keine Wunder zulieb.
Gib deinen Gesetzen recht,
die von Geschlecht zu Geschlecht
sichtbarer sind.

》 》 》

Wenn etwas mir vom Fenster fällt
(und wenn es auch das Kleinste wäre)
wie stürzt sich das Gesetz der Schwere
gewaltig wie ein Wind vom Meere
auf jeden Ball und jede Beere
und trägt sie in den Kern der Welt.

Ein jedes Ding ist überwacht
von einer flugbereiten Güte
wie jeder Stein und jede Blüte

All who seek you put you to the test.
And those who find you tie you
to an image and an act.

But I wish to understand you
like the earth does and bring
with my maturing
into being
you as king.

I want no vanities from you
that prove you exist. I know
that the name of this time and you
are not the same.

Don't perform wonders on my account.
Just be true to the laws you made
which, with every generation,
are harder to debate.

» » »

If something fell off my windowsill
(even if it were the smallest thing),
how pounces there the law of gravity
with vigor, like a gust from the sea,
upon every berry and every ball
and carries them into the deep.

Every single thing is guarded
as by kind wings ready for flight—
every stone is and every flower,

und jedes kleine Kind bei Nacht.
Nur wir, in unsrer Hoffahrt, drängen
aus einigen Zusammenhängen
in einer Freiheit leeren Raum,
statt, klugen Kräften hingegeben,
uns aufzuheben wie ein Baum.
Statt in die weitesten Geleise
sich still und willig einzureihn,
verknüpft man sich auf manche Weise,—
und wer sich ausschließt jedem Kreise,
ist jetzt so namenlos allein.

Da muß er lernen von den Dingen,
anfangen wieder wie ein Kind,
weil sie, die Gott am Herzen hingen,
nicht von ihm fortgegangen sind.
Eins muß er wieder können: *fallen,*
geduldig in der Schwere ruhn,
der sich vermaß, den Vögeln allen
im Fliegen es zuvorzutun.

(Denn auch die Engel fliegen nicht mehr.
Schweren Vögeln gleichen die Seraphim,
welche um *ihn* sitzen und sinnen;
Trümmern von Vögeln, Pinguinen
gleichen sie, wie sie verkümmern. . . .)

» » »

Du meinst die Demut. Angesichter
gesenkt in stillem Dichverstehn.
So gehen abends junge Dichter

and every child at night.
Only we, in our arrogance, push
into the open space to be free
from the few interconnected ties;
instead of yielding to the forces so wise
and going with the flow, as the tree.
Instead of fitting into generous tracks
more willingly and with less dispute,
we seek connectedness with much—
and segregate from each familiar tone
to end up all alone.

Then one will have to start all over again,
start afresh like a child,
become like those things that are close to God
which never left God behind.
Because one dared to imitate
too heavily the flight of birds,
one will have to learn again to fall
and go with gravity's law.

(Even the angels don't fly anymore.
The seraphim resemble heavy birds,
which sit around him in thought;
giants of birds they are,
like penguins, all crippled up. . . .)

» » »

You intend for us to be humble,
with our faces bowed in silent accord
with you, like young poets at night who go

in den entlegenen Alleen.
So stehn die Bauern um die Leiche,
wenn sich ein Kind im Tod verlor,—
und was geschieht, ist doch das Gleiche:
es geht ein Übergroßes vor.

Wer dich zum ersten Mal gewahrt,
den stört der Nachbar und die Uhr,
der geht, gebeugt zu deiner Spur,
und wie beladen und bejahrt.
Erst später naht er der Natur
und fühlt die Winde und die Fernen,
hört dich, geflüstert von der Flur,
sieht dich, gesungen von den Sternen,
und kann dich nirgends mehr verlernen,
und alles ist dein Mantel nur.

Ihm bist du neu und nah und gut
und wunderschön wie eine Reise,
die er in stillen Schiffen leise
auf einem großem Flusse tut.
Das Land ist weit, in Winden, eben,
sehr großen Himmeln preisgegeben
und alten Wäldern untertan.
Die kleinen Dörfer, die sich nahn,
vergehen wieder wie Geläute
und wie ein Gestern und ein Heute
und so wie alles, was wir sahn.
Aber an dieses Stromes Lauf
stehn immer wieder Städte auf
und kommen wie auf Flügelschlägen
der feierlichen Fahrt entgegen.

into distant parks.
Or like sad farmers who surround the child
that was killed; and what happens then
is always the same:
something magnificent rises up.

The one who notices you for the first time
is disturbed by the neighbor and the clock;
he walks bent down to trace your tracks,
like an old person under a heavy weight.
Only later he listens to nature
and senses the winds and plains;
hearing you being whispered from afar,
seeing you, being sung by the stars,
being unable to ever again ignore
you in your coat.

To him you are new and close and kind
and magnificent like a cruise
which he takes on a quiet ship
upon a river great and wide.
The land is far, beyond the sky,
exposed to winds from every place,
and burdened by old woods.
The little hamlets that approach
disperse again like chiming bells—
like yesterday and like today,
and like the rest that we had seen.
But along this river's banks
ever new cities rise into view
and meet us on our festive trip
halfway with whirring wings.

Und manchmal lenkt das Schiff zu Stellen,
die einsam, sonder Dorf und Stadt,
auf etwas warten an den Wellen,—
auf den, der keine Heimat hat. . . .
Für solche stehn dort kleine Wagen
(ein jeder mit drei Pferden vor),
die atemlos nach Abend jagen
auf einem Weg, der sich verlor.

» » »

In diesem Dorfe steht das letzte Haus
so einsam wie das letzte Haus der Welt.

Die Straße, die das kleine Dorf nicht hält,
geht langsam weiter in die Nacht hinaus.

Das kleine Dorf ist nur ein Übergang
zwischen zwei Weiten, ahnungsvoll und bang,
ein Weg an Häusern hin statt eines Stegs.

Und die das Dorf verlassen, wandern lang,
und viele sterben vielleicht unterwegs.

» » »

Manchmal steht einer auf beim Abendbrot
und geht hinaus und geht und geht und geht,—
weil eine Kirche wo im Osten steht.

Und seine Kinder segnen ihn wie tot.

At times the ship steers us to places
secluded, far from city and town,
that wait along the banks—
for those without a home. . . .
For them are hitched up small carriages,
drawn by three horses each
that breathlessly chase after evenings
on a path that later recedes.

》 》 》

In this particular place the very last house
is as lonely as the world's last.

The street, which cannot contain the hamlet,
grows out slowly into the dark.

The hamlet is only a bridge
between two worlds, a foreboding,
a path *alongside* houses, not one straight up.

And those who manage to leave this place
will need to walk for long—or they may die on the way.

》 》 》

Sometimes, at the dinner table, a man might get up
and go outside and walk and walk,
simply because there's somewhere in the East a church.

And his own children consider him dead.

Und einer, welcher stirbt in seinem Haus,
bleibt drinnen wohnen, bleibt in Tisch und Glas,
so daß die Kinder in die Welt hinaus
zu jener Kirche ziehn, die er vergaß.

» » »

Nachtwächter ist der Wahnsinn,
weil er wacht.
Bei jeder Stunde bleibt er lachend stehn,
und einen Namen sucht er für die Nacht
und nennt sie: sieben, achtundzwanzig, zehn. . . .

Und ein Triangel trägt er in der Hand,
und weil er zittert, schlägt es an den Rand
des Horns, das er nicht blasen kann, und singt
das Lied, das er zu allen Häusern bringt.

Die Kinder haben eine gute Nacht
und hören träumend, daß der Wahnsinn wacht.
Die Hunde aber reißen sich vom Ring
und gehen in den Häusern groß umher
und zittern, wenn er schon vorüberging,
und fürchten sich vor seiner Wiederkehr.

» » »

Weißt du von jenen Heiligen, mein Herr?

Sie fühlten auch verschloßne Klosterstuben
zu nahe an Gelächter und Geplärr,
so daß sie tief sich in die Erde gruben.

Yet another, who dies in his own house,
stays put, living on in his table and glass,
so that this time it's the children who walk
to the church their father forgot.

» » »

Folly is a sentinel
who stays awake.
At every hour she lingers and laughs
and she is trying to give the night a name,
and calls it seven, twenty-eight, ten.

And a metal triangle she holds in her hand,
and because she shakes, it clanks to the rim
of the trumpet she cannot sound, and so sings
the song she is carrying to every house.

The children have a very good night
and while dreaming hear how Folly stands guard.
But the dogs break away from their chains
and run about in house and yard
and tremble as she passes
and fear her return.

» » »

Have you heard of those saints, Lord—

Those who felt even the monastery's cell
was too close to laughter and din,
so that they dug themselves in?

Ein jeder atmete mit seinem Licht
die kleine Luft in seiner Grube aus,
vergaß sein Alter und sein Angesicht
und lebte wie ein fensterloses Haus
und starb nichtmehr, als wär er lange tot.

Sie lasen selten; alles war verdorrt,
als wäre Frost in jedes Buch gekrochen,
und wie die Kutte hing von ihren Knochen,
so hing der Sinn herab von jedem Wort.
Sie redeten einander nichtmehr an,
wenn sie sich fühlten in den schwarzen Gängen,
sie ließen ihre langen Haare hängen,
und keiner wußte, ob sein Nachbarmann
nicht stehend starb.
                    In einem runden Raum,
wo Silberlampen sich von Balsam nährten,
versammelten sich manchmal die Gefährten
vor goldnen Türen wie vor goldnen Gärten
und schauten voller Mißtraun in den Traum
und rauschten leise mit den langen Bärten.

Ihr Leben war wie tausend Jahre groß,
seit es sich nichtmehr schied in Nacht und Helle;
sie waren, wie gewälzt von einer Welle,
zurückgekehrt in ihrer Mutter Schooß.
Sie saßen rundgekrümmt wie Embryos
mit großen Köpfen und mit kleinen Händen
und aßen nicht, als ob sie Nahrung fänden
aus jener Erde, die sie schwarz umschloß.

Each one breathed underneath
his light into the little cave,
forgot his looks, forgot his age,
and lived within his sunless house
and ceased to die as if he long were dead.

Their brains were dry, they rarely read,
the frost had crawled into their books;
and like their robes on spindly bones
their words lacked weight and worth.
They no longer spoke to each other,
too busy walking in tunnels, with hair
hanging loose and no one aware
of the brother who might have died
while standing up.
             In a round hall
where silver lamps nibbled on wax
the brothers gathered at times
by golden doors, as in golden yards,
and considered in distrust their dream
and quietly rustled their flowing beards.

Their life was as old as a thousand years
since it no longer distinguished between darkness and light;
they were, as tossed by a wave,
flushed back into their mother's lap.
And so they sat, hunched over like embryos
with giant heads and tiny hands, and didn't eat,
as if they found their food in the soil
into which they had dug themselves deep.

Jetzt zeigt man sie den tausend Pilgern, die
aus Stadt und Steppe zu dem Kloster wallen.
Seit dreimal hundert Jahren liegen sie,
und ihre Leiber können nicht zerfallen.
Das Dunkel häuft sich wie ein Licht das rußt
auf ihren langen lagernden Gestalten,
die unter Tüchern heimlich sich erhalten,—
und ihrer Hände ungelöstes Falten
liegt ihnen wie Gebirge auf der Brust.

Du großer alter Herzog des Erhabnen:
hast du vergessen, diesen Eingegrabnen
den Tod zu schicken, der sie ganz verbraucht,
weil sie sich tief in Erde eingetaucht:
Sind die, die sich Verstorbenen vergleichen,
am ähnlichsten der Unvergänglichkeit?
Ist das das große Leben deiner Leichen,
das überdauern soll den Tod der Zeit?

Sind sie dir noch zu deinen Plänen gut?
Erhältst du unvergängliche Gefäße,
die du, der allen Maßen Ungemäße,
einmal erfüllen willst mit deinem Blut?

» » »

Du bist die Zukunft, großes Morgenrot
über den Ebenen der Ewigkeit.
Du bist der Hahnschrei nach der Nacht der Zeit,
der Tau, die Morgenmette und die Maid,
der fremde Mann, die Mutter und der Tod.

Now, one shows them to the pilgrims who spill
from city and country to the brothers' enclave.
For three hundred years they have been there,
and their bodies cannot find decay.
The dark piles up like a sooting lamp
upon their reclining haggard bodies
that manage to preserve themselves under covers—
and their folded hands, as of yet,
rest like mountains upon their chests.

You great old duke of the lofty skies:
did you forget to send to these buried ones
death that will use them finally up—
them, still stuck into their soil?
Are these who imitate the dead
closest to eternal life?
Is this the kind of life after death
that will last?

Are these dead still of any use to you?
Do you maintain everlasting vessels,
which you, of whom there is no measure,
will fill at one point with your blood?

» » »

You are the future, bright morning red
above the spheres of eternity.
You are the rooster's crow once time is dead;
you are the dew, the matin, and the maid;
you are maverick, mother, death.

Du bist die sich verwandelnde Gestalt,
Die immer einsam aus dem Schicksal ragt,
die unbejubelt bleibt und unbeklagt
und unbeschrieben wie ein wilder Wald.

Du bist der Dinge tiefer Inbegriff,
der seines Wesens letztes Wort verschweigt
und sich den Andern immer anders zeigt:
dem Schiff als Küste und dem Land als Schiff.

» » »

Du bist das Kloster zu den Wundenmalen.
Mit zweiundreißig alten Kathedralen
und fünfzig Kirchen, welche aus Opalen
und Stücken Bernstein aufgemauert sind.
Auf jedem Ding im Klosterhofe
liegt deines Klanges eine Strophe,
und das gewaltige Tor beginnt.

In langen Häusern wohnen Nonnen,
Schwarzschwestern, siebenhundertzehn.
Manchmal kommt eine an den Bronnen,
und eine steht wie eingesponnen,
und eine, wie in Abendsonnen,
geht schlank in schweigsamen Alleen.

Aber die Meisten sieht man nie;
sie bleiben in der Häuser Schweigen
wie in der kranken Brust der Geigen
die Melodie, die keiner kann. . . .

You are the metamorphosis,
who lives apart from happenstance,
so lonely, without fame nor missed,
and nondescript like wilderness.

You are the essence of all things
whose final being is disguised;
who looks to one unlike to another,
to ship as coast, to coast as ship.

» » »

You are the shrine for stigmata,
along with thirty-two cathedrals,
and fifty churches built in bits
of opal, framed by amber beads.
On everything in the abbey's court
are hovering your stanza's words,
and the gate sings them the loudest.

In oblong-shaped houses live the nuns,
black-robed sisters, seven hundred and ten.
One might be walking up to the well,
another stands in thought absorbed,
and one strides with the evening sun
amidst quiet corridors.

But most of them are never seen;
they stay put in their houses so mute,
like an unheard-of melody that rests
in a battered violin's womb.

Und um die Kirche rings im Kreise,
von schmachtenden Jasmin umstellt,
sind Gräberstätten, welche leise
wie Steine reden von der Welt.
Von jener Welt, die nichtmehr ist,
obwohl sie an das Kloster brandet,
ein eitel Tag und Tand gewandet
und gleichbereit zu Lust und List.

Sie ist vergangen: denn du bist.

Sie fließt noch wie ein Spiel von Lichtern
über das teilnahmlose Jahr;
doch dir, dem Abend und den Dichtern
sind, unter rinnenden Gesichtern,
die dunkeln Dinge offenbar.

» » »

Die Könige der Welt sind alt
und werden keine Erben haben.
Die Söhne sterben schon als Knaben,
und ihre bleichen Töchter gaben
die kranken Kronen der Gewalt.

Der Pöbel bricht sie klein zu Geld,
der zeitgemäße Herr der Welt
dehnt sie im Feuer zu Maschinen,
die seinem Wollen grollend dienen;
aber das Glück ist nicht mit ihnen.

And round the churches every which way,
immersed in fragrant jasmine air,
rise tombstones which so softly talk
about a distant world.
They talk of a world that no longer is,
though it ripples against the abbey's walls,
with its vanities and idle talk
and drive for lust and tricks.

This world is past, for you now live.

It still runs like a flickering play
of lights across the passive year;
but to you, to the night and to poets,
the things still hidden, distorted
have now become clear.

» » »

The kings of the world are old
and they will not have heirs.
The sons died as boys,
and the daughters so pale,
yielding to terror, gave their crowns away.

The fool breaks them up for cash,
the modern lord of this world
has them molten into machinery
that serves his whims reluctantly;
but either way, luck is not theirs.

Das Erz hat Heimweh. Und verlassen
will es die Münzen und die Räder,
die es ein kleines Leben lehren.
Und aus Fabriken und aus Kassen
wird es zurück in das Geäder
der aufgetanen Berge kehren,
die sich verschließen hinter ihm.

» » »

Alles wird wieder groß sein und gewaltig.
Die Lande einfach und die Wasser faltig,
die Bäume riesig und sehr klein die Mauern;
und in den Tälern, stark und vielgestaltig,
ein Volk von Hirten und von Ackerbauern.

Und keine Kirchen, welche Gott umklammern
wie einen Flüchtling und ihn dann bejammern
wie ein gefangenes und wundes Tier,—
die Häuser gastlich allen Einlaßklopfern
und ein Gefühl von unbegrenztem Opfern
in allem Handeln und in dir und mir.

Kein Jenseitswarten und kein Schaun nach drüben,
nur Sehnsucht, auch den Tod nicht zu entweihn
und dienend sich am Irdischen zu üben,
um seinen Händen nicht mehr neu zu sein.

» » »   .

Auch du wirst groß sein. Größer noch als einer,
der jetzt schon leben muß, dich sagen kann.

For the metal is homesick and wants to leave
the coins and the cogged wheels,
which lower its quality of life.
And from the factories and cash registers
it will return one day into the veins
of the mountains that will open up
and close again once inside.

» » »

Everything will be magnificent again.
The countryside simple, the waters rippled,
the trees gigantic, the walls dwarfed,
and in the valleys, again distinct and sharp,
will live a herding and farming people.

There will be no churches to pick up God
like a refugee and to pity his lot,
like a captured and wounded animal.
The houses will open to those who knock
and a sense of unlimited giving will prevail
in all activity, and in you and me.

No more waiting for the beyond, no looking hither,
only a desire not to minimize death and to train
for service on the things earthly
so as to be ready and of good use to them.

» » »

Even you, God, will be big. Bigger than the one
who lives now and reveals himself.

Viel ungewöhnlicher und ungemeiner
und noch viel älter als ein alter Mann.

Man wird dich fühlen: daß ein Duften ginge
aus eines Gartens naher Gegenwart;
und wie ein Kranker seine liebsten Dinge
wird man dich lieben ahnungsvoll und zart.

Es wird kein Beten geben, das die Leute
zusammenschart. Du *bist* nicht im Verein;
und wer dich fühlte und sich an dir freute,
wird wie der Einzige auf Erden sein:
Ein Ausgestoßner und ein Vereinter,
gesammelt und vergeudet doch zugleich;
ein Lächelnder und doch ein Halbverweinter,
klein wie ein Haus und mächtig wie ein Reich.

» » »

Es wird nicht Ruhe in den Häusern, sei's
daß einer stirbt und sie ihn weitertragen,
sei es daß wer auf heimliches Geheiß
den Pilgerstock nimmt und den Pilgerkragen,
um in der Fremde nach dem Weg zu fragen,
auf welchem er dich warten weiß.

Die Straßen werden derer niemals leer,
die zu dir wollen wie zu jener Rose,
die alle tausend Jahre einmal blüht.
Viel dunkles Volk und beinah Namenlose,
und wenn sie dich erreichen, sind sie müd.

Much more unusual and extraordinary
and much older than an Ancient One.

One will notice you like a fragrance
wafting from a yard nearby;
and like a patient treasuring a few select things,
one will love you with heart and mind.

There will be no more prayer in a crowd.
For you are not found
in a club. And whoever tasted you with delight
will think himself the only one alive:
Both as one expelled and one united,
one preserved and one dissipated,
one smiling, though with tears afloat,
one modest like a hut and mighty like a fort.

» » »

There will never be apathy in the homes,
either because someone will die and be carried on,
or someone will respond to the secret calling
of a pilgrimage, with staff and hooded cloak,
asking directions on the path abroad
to where you are waiting.

The streets will never be devoid of those
who journey to you, a magnificent rose
that only once a millennium blooms.
There will be a lot of plain-looking, almost nameless folk,
and once they reach you, they are tired out.

Aber ich habe ihren Zug gesehn;
und glaube seither, daß die Winde wehn
aus ihren Mänteln, welche sich bewegen,
und stille sind wenn sie sich niederlegen—:
so groß war in den Ebenen ihr Gehn.

» » »

So möcht ich zu dir gehn: von fremden Schwellen
Almosen sammelnd, die mich ungern nähren.
Und wenn der Wege wirrend viele wären,
so würd ich mich den Ältesten gesellen.
Ich würde mich zu kleinen Greisen stellen,
und wenn sie gingen, schaut ich wie im Traum,
daß ihre Kniee aus der Bärte Wellen
wie Inseln tauchen, ohne Strauch und Baum.

Wir überholten Männer, welche blind
mit ihren Knaben wie mit Augen schauen,
und Trinkende am Fluß und müde Frauen
und viele Frauen, welche schwanger sind.
Und alle waren mir so seltsam nah,—
als ob die Männer einen Blutsverwandten,
die Frauen einen Freund in mir erkannten,
und auch die Hunde kamen, die ich sah.

» » »

Du Gott, ich möchte viele Pilger sein,
um so, ein langer Zug, zu dir zu gehn,
und um ein großes Stück von dir zu sein:
du Garten mit den lebenden Alleen.

But I have seen their throng and know
since then that the winds blow
when their cloaks are moving
and are still when they lie down—
that's how powerful is their walking.

» » »

And that's how I want to journey to you, live
on alms from those who reluctantly give.
And if the paths were confusingly many,
I would consult the elders there.
I would mingle with these little, old folk,
and once they walked on, I'd be aware
of how from amidst their wavy beards their knees
emerged like islands bare.

We would pass the blind led by young eyes;
we would pass the thirsty by the river,
women who were tired,
and many women big with child.
To all of them I would be strangely close,
as if the men viewed me as next of kin,
as if the women found in me a friend,
and dogs I saw would all come up.

» » »

O God, I want to be many pilgrims at once,
be a train like that journeying on
to you, and be a larger share of you than this:
you garden of what walks and lives.

Wenn ich so geh wie ich bin, allein,—
wer merkt es denn? Wer *sieht* mich zu dir gehn?
Wen reißt es hin? Wen regt es auf, und wen
bekehrt es dir?
                    Als wäre nichts geschehn,
—lachen sie weiter. Und da bin ich froh,
daß ich so gehe wie ich bin; denn so
kann keiner von den Lachenden mich sehn.

» » »

Bei Tag bist du das Hörensagen,
das flüsternd um die Vielen fließt;
die Stille nach dem Stundenschlagen,
welche sich langsam wieder schließt.

Jemehr der Tag mit immer schwächern
Gebärden sich nach Abend neigt,
jemehr bist du, mein Gott. Es steigt
dein Reich wie Rauch aus allen Dächern.

» » »

Ein Pilgermorgen. Von den harten Lagern,
auf das ein jeder wie vergiftet fiel,
erhebt sich bei dem ersten Glockenspiel
ein Volk von hagern Morgensegen-Sagern,
auf das die frühe Sonne niederbrennt:

Bärtige Männer, welche sich verneigen,
Kinder, die ernsthaft aus den Pelzen steigen,
und in den Mänteln, schwer von ihrem Schweigen,

When I wander on my own, who knows that I do?
Who sees me walking to you?
Who is touched by it, who appalled,
and who is turned around and found?
But as if nothing had happened, they keep
on giggling. Though a good thing it is,
so I too can carry on like I did before,
and the gigglers won't know.

» » »

By day you are but secondhand sound,
which mills about creation in a hum;
you are the stillness when the bells have rung
that gently folds itself around.

But the more the hours come to a close
in ever more sluggish moves,
the more you are, O God. Your rule
drifts up like smoke from roofs.

» » »

It's morning on the pilgrimage.
From stone-hard mats on which one slept
like dead, one rises with the steeples' chimes—
a people of haggard morning blessers
on whom the morning sun lies:

There are bearded men uttering blessings,
children emerging from furs,
and, wrapped in cloaks and quiet,

die braunen Fraun von Tiflis und Taschkent.
Christen mit den Gebärden des Islam
sind um die Brunnen, halten ihre Hände
wie flache Schalen hin, wie Gegenstände,
in die die Flut wie eine Seele kam.

Sie neigen das Gesicht hinein und trinken,
reißen die Kleider auf mit ihrer Linken
und halten sich das Wasser an die Brust
als wärs ein kühles weinendes Gesicht,
das von den Schmerzen auf der Erde spricht.

Und diese Schmerzen stehen rings umher
mit welken Augen; und du weißt nicht wer
sie sind und waren. Knechte oder Bauern,
vielleicht Kaufleute, welche Wohlstand sahn,
vielleicht auch laue Mönche, die nicht dauern,
und Diebe, die auf die Versuchung lauern,
offene Mädchen, die verkümmert kauern,
und Irrende in einem Wald von Wahn—:
alle wie Fürsten, die in tiefem Trauern
die Überflüsse von sich abgetan.
Wie Weise all, welche viel erfahren,
Erwählte, welche in der Wüste waren,
wo Gott sie nährte durch ein fremdes Tier;
Einsame, die durch Ebenen gegangen
mit vielen Winden an den dunklen Wangen,
von einer Sehnsucht fürchtig und befangen
und doch so wundersam erhöht von ihr.
Gelöste aus dem Alltag, eingeschaltet
in große Orgeln und in Chorgesang,
und Kniende, wie Steigende gestaltet;

the brunettes of large Russian cities.
They are Christians with the gestures of Islam
gathered round the well, hands held up
like objects, as cups and plates,
to catch the spirit's flood.

With faces immersed they drink,
with their left hand tearing open the shirt
and splashing water onto their chest
as if it were a tear-drenched face
that tells of the pain in the world.

This pain forms a circle of watery eyes;
you wonder who these people are or have been:
Farmhands or farmers, perhaps
merchants who once had seen wealth,
perhaps lukewarm monks who will not persist;
or thieves, awaiting their turn with stealth;
loose women, cowering now in corners;
and those confused by their own insanity;
all like princes who in their agony
renounced the extras that they did not need.
Like the wise who have been through much,
chosen ones, whom the desert touched,
where God had them fed by strange beasts;
lonely ones, who walked the wilderness
with many gusts on their hollow cheeks,
awed and captivated by a longing
and still so wondrously enthralled by it.
Detached they are from everyday life,
infused into choirs and giant organs;
kneeling ones who look as though they climbed;

Fahnen mit Bildern, welche lang
verborgen waren und zusammengefaltet:

Jetzt hängen sie sich langsam wieder aus.

Und manche stehn und schaun nach einem Haus,
darin die Pilger, welche krank sind, wohnen;
denn eben wand sich dort ein Mönch heraus,
die Haare schlaff und die Sutane kraus,
das schattige Gesicht voll kranker Blaus
und ganz verdunkelt von Dämonen.

Er neigte sich als bräch er sich entzwei,
und warf sich in zwei Stücken auf die Erde,
die jetzt an seinem Munde wie ein Schrei
zu hängen schien und so als sei
sie seiner Arme wachsende Gebärde.

Und langsam ging sein Fall an ihm vorbei.

Er flog empor, als ob er Flügel spürte,
und sein erleichtertes Gefühl verführte
ihn zu dem Glauben seiner Vogelwerdung.
Er hing in seinen magern Armen schmal,
wie eine schiefgeschobene Marionette,
und glaubte, daß er große Schwingen hätte
und daß die Welt schon lange wie ein Tal
sich ferne unter seinen Füßen glätte.
Ungläubig sah er sich mit einem Mal
herabgelassen auf die fremde Stätte
und auf den grünen Meergrund seiner Qual.
Und war ein Fisch und wand sich schlank und schwamm

symbol-bearing banners, wrapped up
and stashed away for long:

But now they are slowly unfolding.

One might be looking at the place
where pilgrims struck by sickness stay;
a monk just dragged himself from there,
his cowl all crumpled, with flattened hair,
the haggard face of a bluish cast,
possessed by powers of the dark.

Then he was bending over, as if to split
open in two, and threw himself to the ground,
which seemed to cling now to his mouth
like a scream and blended
with his arms extended.

And slowly the attack did pass.

And he rose up, as if lifted by wings,
and his relief was tempting him
to consider himself a bird.
With his bony arms suspended
and dangling like a marionette,
he thought he had wide wings
and that the world was leveling
as a vale far below his feet.
But then in disbelief he saw
himself being lowered to strange soil,
the green, wet bottom of his pain.
And he was fish and dived and swam

durch tiefes Wasser, still und silbergrau.
Sah Quallen hangen am Korallenstamm
und sah die Haare einer Meerjungfrau,
durch die das Wasser rauschte wie ein Kamm.
Und kam zu Land und war ein Bräutigam
bei einer Toten, wie man ihn erwählt
damit kein Mädchen fremd und unvermählt
des Paradieses Wiesenland beschritte.

Er folgte ihr und ordnete die Tritte
und tanzte rund, sie immer in der Mitte,
und seine Arme tanzten rund um ihn.

Dann horchte er, als wäre eine dritte
Gestalt ganz sachte in das Spiel getreten,
die diesem Tanzen nicht zu glauben schien.
Und da erkannte er: jetzt mußt du beten;
denn dieser ist es, welcher den Propheten
wie eine große Krone sich verliehn.
Wir halten ihn, um den wir täglich flehten,
wir ernten ihn, den einstens Ausgesäeten,
und kehren heim mit ruhenden Geräten
in langen Reihen wie in Melodien.
Und er verneigte sich ergriffen, tief.

Aber der Alte war, als ob er schliefe,
und sah es nicht, obwohl sein Aug nicht schlief.

Und er verneigte sich in solche Tiefe,
daß ihm ein Zittern durch die Glieder lief.
Aber der Alte ward es nicht gewahr.

through waters deep, and smooth and gray,
saw jellyfish cling to coral reefs
and even noted a mermaid's hair,
for which the waters were a comb.
And reached the land and was a groom
to someone dead, the way it's done
so that no maiden should alone
step on the leas of Eden.

He followed her with measured steps
and danced around her, while his arms
danced too, around himself.

But there he perceived that someone else,
a third, had tiptoed on the scene,
who didn't seem to like the dance.
And then he knew: You need to pray;
for this is he who lent himself
to prophets as their crown.
We are holding him, for whom we daily plead;
we are reaping him, who once was seed;
and we go back home with tools that rest
in rows, like melodies.
And the monk in awe bowed deep.

But the Ancient One must have been asleep,
despite his one open eye.

And then the monk bowed with such a passion
that his entire body shook.
But the Ancient One still didn't look.

Da faßte sich der kranke Mönch am Haar
und schlug sich wie ein Kleid an einen Baum.
Aber der Alte stand und sah es kaum.

Da nahm der kranke Mönch sich in die Hände
wie man ein Richtschwert in die Hände nimmt,
und hieb und hieb, verwundete die Wände
und stieß sich endlich in den Grund ergrimmt.
Aber der Alte blickte unbestimmt.

Da riß der Mönch sein Kleid sich ab wie Rinde
und knieend hielt er es dem Alten hin.
Und sieh: er kam. Kam wie zu einem Kinde
und sagte sanft: Weißt du auch *wer ich bin?*
Das wußte er. Und legte sich gelinde
dem Greis wie eine Geige unters Kinn.

» » »

Jetzt reifen schon die roten Berberitzen,
alternde Astern atmen schwach im Beet.
Wer jetzt nicht reich ist, da der Sommer geht,
wird immer warten und sich nie besitzen.

Wer jetzt nicht seine Augen schließen kann,
gewiß, daß eine Fülle von Gesichten
in ihm nur wartet bis die Nacht begann,
um sich in seinem Dunkel aufzurichten:—
der ist vergangen wie ein alter Mann.

Dem kommt nichts mehr, dem stößt kein Tag mehr zu,
und alles lügt ihn an, was ihm geschieht;

So then the monk clutched strands of his hair
and hit his head near flat against a tree.
The Ancient One stood and barely did see.

So then the monk grasped his own limbs,
the way one holds an executioner's ax,
and hit and hit, and marred the walls,
and pegged his body down half crazed.
The Ancient One indistinctly gazed.

Then the monk tore off his robe like bark
and knelt and held it up to him.
And see—the Ancient One came. Came like to a child
and gently said: Are you aware of who I am?
He knew, this monk, and like a violin
lay down beneath his chin.

» » »

The red barberries are about to ripen,
the old chrysanthemums heave.
Whoever is not rich by summer's end
will never find nor find himself.

Whoever cannot close his eyes then,
assured of the fullness of visions
and waiting for the night to begin
to be uplifted by them, is indeed
an old man.

He will never receive, no day will hold a surprise,
and everything he considers blatant lies;

auch du, mein Gott. Und wie ein Stein bist du,
welcher ihn täglich in die Tiefe zieht.

» » »

Du mußt nicht bangen, Gott. Sie sagen: *mein*
zu allen Dingen, die geduldig sind.
Sie sind wie Wind der an die Zweige streift
und sagt: *mein* Baum.

Sie merken kaum,
wie alles glüht, was ihre Hand ergreift,—
so daß sie's auch an seinem letzten Saum
nicht halten könnten ohne zu verbrennen.

Sie sagen *mein,* wie manchmal einer gern
den Fürsten Freund nennt im Gespräch mit Bauern,
wenn dieser Fürst sehr groß ist und—sehr fern.
Sie sagen *mein* von ihren fremden Mauern
und kennen gar nicht ihres Hauses Herrn.
Sie sagen *mein* und nennen das Besitz,
wenn jedes Ding sich schließt, dem sie sich nahn,
so wie ein abschmackter Charlatan
vielleicht die Sonne sein nennt und den Blitz.
So sagen sie: mein Leben, meine Frau,
mein Hund, mein Kind, und wissen doch genau,
daß alles: Leben, Frau und Hund und Kind
fremde Gebilde sind, daran sie blind
mit ihren ausgestreckten Händen stoßen.
Gewißheit freilich ist das nur den Großen,
die sich nach Augen sehnen. Denn die Andern
wollens nicht hören, daß ihr armes Wandern

even you, dear Lord. And you become a stone
to him, one that drags him down.

» » »

Don't worry, God. They call "mine"
everything that is patient.
They are like the wind brushing the branch
and saying: *my* tree.

They hardly see
the glow of all they touch—
unaware that they couldn't even hold its outer edge
without burning up.

They say "mine" like someone calling the prince
a friend during a chat with farmers in town,
especially when the prince is great—and far gone.
They call "mine" their walls of stone,
but do not know the Lord of their home.
They say "mine" and call it theirs although
everything withdraws when they approach,
like a boisterous charlatan
might call his the lightning and the sun.
That's why they say: my life, my wife,
my dog, my child, and know quite well
that everything—life, wife, dog, and child—
is someone else's work on which
they scrape their groping hands.
Certainty is only reserved for the wise,
those longing for eyes.
The rest will not hear that their being

mit keinem Dinge rings zusammenhängt,
daß sie, von ihrer Habe fortgedrängt,
nicht anerkannt von ihrem Eigentume,
das Weib so wenig *haben* wie die Blume,
die eines fremden Lebens ist für alle.

Falle nicht, Gott, aus deinem Gleichgewicht.
Auch der dich liebt und der dein Angesicht
erkennt im Dunkel, wenn er wie ein Licht
in deinem Atem schwankt,—besitzt dich nicht.
Und wenn dich einer in der Nacht erfaßt,
so daß du kommen mußt in sein Gebet:
      Du bist der Gast,
         der wieder weiter geht.

Wer kann dich halten, Gott? Denn du bist dein,
von keines Eigentümers Hand gestört,
so wie der noch nicht ausgereifte Wein,
der immer süßer wird, sich selbst gehört.

» » »

In tiefen Nächten grab ich dich, du Schatz.
Denn alle Überflüsse, die ich sah,
sind Armut und armsäliger Ersatz
für deine Schönheit, die noch nie geschah.

Aber der Weg zu dir ist furchtbar weit
und, weil ihn lange keiner ging, verweht.
O du bist einsam. Du bist Einsamkeit,
du Herz, das zu entfernten Talen geht.

is not connected to anything;
that they, rejected by hearth and home
and unacknowledged by their belongings,
own their wife as little as the flower,
which owns itself alone.

You will not lose your balance, God.
Even the one who loves you and can
make out your face in the dark and lift
his light near your breath
does not possess you. And if
one were to seize you by praying hard:

       You are the guest
       who will depart.

Who can really hold on to you, God?
For you are yours alone, no owners there
that might disturb; just like young wine
turns sweeter by itself and is its own.

》 》 》

In long nights I dig for you, you gold.
For every luxury I knew is poverty
and spurious substitute for the beauty
you have yet to show.

But the path to you is terribly far and hid
since for so long no one has walked on it.
You are alone. You are solitude, my love,
walking amidst deep and distant lots.

Und meine Hände, welche blutig sind
vom Graben, heb ich offen in den Wind,
so daß sie sich verzweigen wie ein Baum.
Ich sauge dich mit ihnen aus dem Raum
als hättest du dich einmal dort zerschellt
in einer ungeduldigen Gebärde,
und fielest jetzt, eine zerstäubte Welt,
aus fernen Sternen wieder auf die Erde
sanft wie ein Frühlingsregen fällt.

From digging my hands are covered by blood
and I openly raise them up,
so they branch out like a tree
and absorb you from the air,
as if you were shattered there
by a rash move you made, an accident;
and were now about to descend
in fine particles from distant stars,
like spring rains, unto earth.

» » » Das Buch von der Armut und vom Tode

Vielleicht, daß ich durch schwere Berge gehe
in harten Adern, wie ein Erz allein;
und bin so tief, daß ich kein Ende sehe
und keine Ferne: alles wurde Nähe
und alle Nähe wurde Stein.

Ich bin ja noch kein Wissender im Wehe,—
so macht mich dieses große Dunkel klein;
bist *Du* es aber: mach mich schwer, brich ein:
daß deine ganze Hand an mir geschehe
und ich an dir mit meinem ganzen Schrein.

» » »

Du Berg, der blieb da die Gebirge kamen,—
Hang ohne Hütten, Gipfel ohne Namen,
ewiger Schnee, in dem die Sterne lahmen,
und Träger jener Tale der Cyclamen,
aus denen aller Duft der Erde geht;
du, aller Berge Mund und Minaret
(von dem noch nie der Abendruf erschallte):

Geh ich in dir jetzt? Bin ich im Basalte
wie ein noch ungefundenes Metall?
Ehrfürchtig füll ich deine Felsenspalte,
und deine Härte fühl ich überall.

» » » The Book of Poverty and Death

THIRD BOOK, 1903

Like a piece of solitary ore
I may be crawling through mountainous veins
and am so deep there is no end anymore:
everything is close up,
and every closeness has become rock.

I'm still a novice concerning pain—
that's how small I feel in this great dark;
but if you are there, be heavy and break through;
have your whole hand do its work on me
and I, with my cries, on you.

» » »

You mountain who remained as the highlands formed—
slope without huts, ridge without name,
eternal snow where the stars grow lame,
and bearer of those valleys of cyclamen
from which issue all aromas of the earth;
you mouth and minaret of every mountain
(from which the evening prayer call was never heard):

Am I walking inside you? Am I in lava rock
like a metal still unmined?
With deference I fill in your crevices
and am by your hardness entwined.

Oder ist das die Angst, in der ich bin?
die tiefe Angst der übergroßen Städte,
in die du mich gestellt hast bis ans Kinn?

O daß dir einer recht geredet hätte
von ihres Wesens Wahn und Abersinn.
Du stündest auf, du Sturm aus Anbeginn,
und triebest sie wie Hülsen vor dir hin. . . .

Und willst du jetzt von mir: so rede recht,—
so bin ich nichtmehr Herr in meinem Munde,
der nichts als zugehn will wie eine Wunde;
und meine Hände halten sich wie Hunde
an meinen Seiten, jedem Ruf zu schlecht.

Du zwingst mich, Herr, zu einer fremden Stunde.

» » »

Mach mich zum Wächter deiner Weiten,
mach mich zum Horchenden am Stein,
gib mir die Augen auszubreiten
auf deiner Meere Einsamsein;
laß mich der Flüsse Gang begleiten
aus dem Geschrei zu beiden Seiten
weit in den Klang der Nacht hinein.

Schick mich in deine leeren Länder,
durch die die weiten Winde gehn,
wo große Klöster wie Gewänder
um ungelebte Leben stehn.
Dort will ich mich zu Pilgern halten,

Or is it fear in which I live?
the fear of the teeming cities,
where you placed me deep?

If only someone protested to you on their behalf,
of their madness and their erratic ways.
You would rise, you who were storm from the start,
and toss them up and ahead of you like chaff.

If you would like to enlist me, tell me now—
so I will surrender the right to my mouth
and have it seal up like a wound
and keep my hands straight down,
like dogs that mind and stay close.

You force me into this pose.

» » »

Make me the guardian of your estate,
make me the listener upon the rock,
give me the eyes to spread across
your seas of loneliness;
allow me to pair up with the rivers' flow
and flee from the screaming on either side
and drift into the sound of night.

Send me into your desert lands
through which blow the widening winds,
where the big cloisters stand
around lives unlived.
There I will keep near the faithful,

von ihren Stimmen und Gestalten
durch keinen Trug mehr abgetrennt,
und hinter einem blinden Alten
des Weges gehn, den keiner kennt.

» » »

Denn, Herr, die großen Städte sind
verlorene und aufgelöste;
wie Flucht vor Flammen ist die größte,—
und ist kein Trost, daß er sie tröste,
und ihre kleine Zeit verrinnt.

Da leben Menschen, leben schlecht und schwer,
in tiefen Zimmern, bange von Gebärde,
geängsteter denn eine Erstlingsherde;
und draußen wacht und atmet deine Erde,
sie aber sind und wissen es nicht mehr.

Da wachsen Kinder auf an Fensterstufen,
die immer in demselben Schatten sind,
und wissen nicht, daß draußen Blumen rufen
zu einem Tag voll Weite, Glück und Wind,—
und müssen Kind sein und sind traurig Kind.

Da blühen Jungfraun auf zum Unbekannten
und sehnen sich nach ihrer Kindheit Ruh;
das aber ist nicht da, wofür sie brannten,
und zitternd schließen sie sich wieder zu.
Und haben in verhüllten Hinterzimmern
die Tage der enttäuschten Mutterschaft,
der langen Nächte willenloses Wimmern

undistracted by self-deception
from their countenance and voice,
and behind a blind old man
I will follow the path no one knows.

» » »

For Lord, the major big cities are
desperate and disjointed,
the biggest resembling an escape from flames—
deserted by solace to comfort her
and her little time left runs out.

People are living there poorly and grave,
in basement rooms, small and confined,
more timid than a firstborn herd;
and while outside your earth awakes to breathe,
they are unaware they too do live.

Children grow up in window wells,
ever dipped into perpetual shade,
and don't know that flowers are calling outside
to a day so wide and sweeping and glad—
and are forced to be children, and are children so sad.

Young women unfold blossoms unto the unknown
and desire the peace they had as girls;
but what they so burned for never appears
and so they again close up.
And they store in their back rooms, veiled,
the days of their disappointing motherhood;
the unwitting whimpers during long nights,

und kalte Jahre ohne Kampf und Kraft.
Und ganz im Dunkel stehn die Sterbebetten,
und langsam sehnen sie sich dazu hin;
und sterben lange, sterben wie in Ketten
und gehen aus wie eine Bettlerin.

» » »

Da leben Menschen, weißerblühte, blasse,
und sterben staunend an der schweren Welt.
Und keiner sieht die klaffende Grimasse,
zu der das Lächeln einer zarten Rasse
in namenlosen Nächten sich entstellt.

Sie gehn umher, entwürdigt durch die Müh,
sinnlosen Dingen ohne Mut zu dienen,
und ihre Kleider werden welk an ihnen,
und ihre schönen Hände altern früh.

Die Menge drängt und denkt nicht sie zu schonen,
obwohl sie etwas zögernd sind und schwach,—
nur scheue Hunde, welche nirgends wohnen,
gehn ihnen leise eine Weile nach.

Sie sind gegeben unter hundert Quäler,
und, angeschrien von jeder Stunde Schlag,
kreisen sie einsam um die Hospitäler
und warten angstvoll auf den Einlaßtag.

Dort ist der Tod. Nicht jener, dessen Grüße
sie in der Kindheit wundersam gestreift,—
der kleine Tod, wie man ihn dort begreift;

and the empty years without strength and fight.
With the deathbeds way back in the dark,
they now begin to long for them;
and they die slowly, die like in chains,
and, like a beggar woman, depart.

» » »

People live there white blossomed and pale
and die amazed at the world's plight.
And no one sees the gaping grimaces
into which the smiles of such a tender race
of people turned in nameless nights.

They walk about, degraded by their work,
serving meaningless things without desire;
and their dress begins to droop,
and their pretty hands age early on.

Greed wastes no thought of sparing them,
though they are weary and worn out—
only roaming dogs without home
follow them on occasion around.

Unto a hundred torturers they have been delivered
and, screamed at by each hour's strike,
they make their lonely rounds about the hospitals
and wait for their admittance there with fright.

That's where death is. Not the one striking
in their childhood mysteriously from afar—
not death as known back then, so small;

ihr eigener hängt grün und ohne Süße
wie eine Frucht in ihnen, die nicht reift.

» » »

O Herr, gib jedem seinen eigenen Tod.
Das Sterben, das aus jenem Leben geht,
darin er Liebe hatte, Sinn und Not.

» » »

Denn wir sind nur die Schale und das Blatt.
Der große Tod, den jeder in sich hat,
das ist die Frucht, um die sich alles dreht.
Um ihretwillen heben Mädchen an
und kommen wie ein Baum aus einer Laute,
und Knaben sehnen sich um sie zum Mann;
und Frauen sind den Wachsenden Vertraute
für Ängste, die sonst niemand nehmen kann.
Um ihretwillen *bleibt* das Angeschaute
wie Ewiges, auch wenn es lang verrann,—
und jeder, welcher bildete und baute,
ward Welt um diese Frucht, und fror und taute
und windete ihr zu und schien sie an.
In sie ist eingegangen alle Wärme
der Herzen und der Hirne weißes Glühn—:
Doch deine Engel ziehn wie Vogelschwärme,
und sie erfanden alle Früchte grün.

» » »

Herr: Wir sind ärmer denn die armen Tiere,
die ihres Todes enden, wennauch blind,

but one that hangs in them like a piece of fruit,
green and sour, refusing to mature.

» » »

O Lord, grant death to each in one's own way.
Grant that one may pass away from a life
that was filled with love, meaning, and desire.

» » »

For we are only hull and leaf.
The large death, which each carries within,
is the fruit around which it all spins.
For its sake alone the girls start songs
and rise like a tree from a lute,
and boys long for its sake to be men;
and women care for those growing up
steeped in fears no one else would bear.
The visible remains, for its sake alone,
eternal, even when gone—
and everyone who built and formed
was world around this fruit, and froze
and melted and turned and lighted it up.
Into this fruit went the warmth of every heart
and the glowing embers of the mind—
yet your angels flying in bird colonies
kept finding the fruit not yet ripe.

» » »

Lord, we are poorer than beasts,
which, though unaware, at least can die;

weil wir noch alle ungestorben sind.
Den gib uns, der die Wissenschaft gewinnt,
das Leben aufzubinden in Spaliere,
um welche zeitiger der Mai beginnt.

Denn dieses macht das Sterben fremd und schwer,
daß es nicht *unser* Tod ist; einer der
uns endlich nimmt, nur weil wir keinen reifen.
Drum geht ein Sturm, uns alle abzustreifen.

Wir stehn in deinem Garten Jahr und Jahr
und sind die Bäume, süßen Tod zu tragen;
aber wir altern in den Erntetagen,
und so wie Frauen, welche du geschlagen,
sind wir verschlossen, schlecht und unfruchtbar.
Oder ist meine Hoffahrt ungerecht:
sind Bäume besser? Sind wir nur Geschlecht
und Schooß von Frauen, welche viel gewähren?—
Wir haben mit der Ewigkeit gehurt,
und wenn das Kreißbett da ist, so gebären
wir unsres Todes tote Fehlgeburt;
den krummen, kummervollen Embryo,
der sich (als ob ihn Schreckliches erschreckte)
die Augenkeime mit den Händen deckte
und dem schon auf der ausgebauten Stirne
die Angst von allem steht, was er nicht litt,—
und alle schließen so wie eine Dirne
in Kindbettkrämpfen und am Kaiserschnitt.

» » »

Mach Einen herrlich, Herr, mach Einen groß,
bau seinem Leben einen schönen Schooß,

for we can only die halfway.
Give us the one who can manage
the staking of life on a trellis
so May can much sooner arrive.

Death is so foreign and grave,
because it's not ours, but one who takes us
only because we couldn't grow our own,
and sweeps us away like a storm.

We stand in your yard year in, year out,
are trees intent to bear death sweet and ripe;
but when harvesttime comes,
we are like women you struck
barren, infertile, and dark.
With my attestations I might be unjust:
Are trees not better? Are we not vagina
and lap of women, who give in too much?
We have been whoring with eternity
and in labor we only give birth
by miscarriage to our own death;
a dead, crippled, miserable embryo,
who uses (as if terribly frightened)
his hands to hide the sockets of his eyes
and on his already prominent brow
stands fear of a pain it never bore—
thus everybody dies like whores
in labor pain and with Caesarean sections.

» » »

Raise up one, Lord, who is glorious and great
and build a beautiful home for him;

und seine Scham errichte wie ein Tor
in einem blonden Wald von jungen Haaren,
und ziehe durch das Glied des Unsagbaren
den Reisigen, den weißen Heeresscharen,
den tausend Samen, die sich sammeln, vor.

Und eine Nacht gib, daß der Mensch empfinge
was keines Menschen Tiefen noch betrat;
gib eine Nacht: da blühen alle Dinge,
und mach sie duftender als die Syringe
und wiegender denn deines Windes Schwinge
und jubelnder als Josaphat.

Und gib ihm eines langen Tragens Zeit
und mach ihn weit in wachsenden Gewändern,
und schenk ihm eines Sternes Einsamkeit,
daß keines Auges Staunen ihn beschreit,
wenn seine Züge schmelzend sich verändern.

Erneue ihn mit einer reinen Speise,
mit Tau, mit ungetötetem Gericht,
mit jenem Leben, das wie Andacht leise
und warm wie Atem aus den Feldern bricht.

Mach, daß er seine Kindheit wieder weiß;
das Unbewußte und das Wunderbare
und seiner ahnungsvollen Anfangsjahre
unendlich dunkelreichen Sagenkreis.

Und also heiß ihn seiner Stunde warten,
da er den Tod gebären wird, den Herrn:

construct his shame like a towering gate
in a blond forest of youthful hair;
and give preference in an unheard-of act
to this warrior over all angelic hosts
and the thousands of seeds that collect.

Give just one night where this person can absorb
the depth where no one else trod;
give one night, where all is in bloom
more fragrant than the mock orange shrub
and more soothing than the wind's rush
and more jubilant than Jehoshaphat.

And give him time to mature for long
and make him wide in a growing garb
and lend him the loneliness of an entire star,
so no inquisitive eye will stare
when his expressions transform.

Restore him with a dish that is pure,
with dew, with nothing that had to be killed,
with the life that like worship seeps
calm and warm from the fields.

Arrange it so his childhood comes back;
the unconscious and the wonderful
and the infinitely rich cycle of lore
of his early prescient years.

And call on him to wait for his hour
when he will bring forth death, the lord:

allein und rauschend wie ein großer Garten,
und ein Versammelter aus fern.

» » »

Das letzte Zeichen laß an uns geschehen,
erscheine in der Krone deiner Kraft,
und gib uns jetzt (nach aller Weiber Wehen)
des Menschen ernste Mutterschaft.
Erfülle, du gewaltiger Gewährer,
nicht jenen Traum der Gottgebärerin,—
richt auf den Wichtigen: den Tod-Gebärer,
und führ uns mitten durch die Hände derer,
die ihn verfolgen werden, zu ihm hin.
Denn sieh, ich sehe seine Widersacher,
und sie sind mehr als Lügen in der Zeit,—
und er wird aufstehn in dem Land der Lacher
und wird ein Träumer heißen: denn ein Wacher
ist immer Träumer unter Trunkenheit.

Du aber gründe ihn in deine Gnade,
in deinem alten Glanze pflanz ihn ein;
und mich laß Tänzer dieser Bundeslade,
laß mich den Mund der neuen Messiade,
den Tönenden, den Täufer sein.

» » »

Ich will ihn preisen. Wie vor einem Heere
die Hörner gehen, will ich gehn und schrein.
Mein Blut soll lauter rauschen denn die Meere,
mein Wort soll süß sein, daß man sein begehre,
und doch nicht irre machen wie der Wein.

alone and rustling like a big yard,
one that has been summoned from afar.

》》》

But let the final round happen to us:
appear at the height of your might,
and give to us (after all these labor pains)
a motherhood that is true.
Do not fulfill, you mighty giver,
the dream of the woman birthing God—
raise up the important one instead:
the one giving birth to death
and lead us by the hands of those that follow him.
Now see, I notice his foes,
and they are more than recurring lies;
in the land of mockers he will rise
and will be called a dreamer: for someone awake
will always be called a dreamer by the dazed.

So place him in your mercy;
amidst your ancient glory plant him firm;
and me, make me the dancer around this ark,
make me the mouth of this messianic pact,
and singer and baptizer.

》》》

I want to praise him. As before a troop
the horns are carried, I will go and shout.
My blood shall rush much louder than the seas,
my speech be sweet so that one longs for it,
yet not bedazzle as does wine.

Und in den Frühlingsnächten, wenn nicht viele
geblieben sind um meine Lagerstatt,
dann will ich blühn in meinem Saitenspiele
so leise wie die nördlichen Aprile,
die spät und ängstlich sind um jedes Blatt.

Denn meine Stimme wuchs nach zweien Seiten
und ist ein Duften worden und ein schrein:
die eine will den Fernen vorbereiten,
die andere muß meiner Einsamkeiten
Gesicht und Seligkeit und Engel sein.

» » »

Und gib, daß beide Stimmen mich begleiten,
streust du mich wieder aus in Stadt und Angst.
Mit ihnen will ich sein im Zorn der Zeiten,
und dir aus meinem Klang ein Bett bereiten
an jeder Stelle, wo du es verlangst.

» » »

Die großen Städte sind nicht wahr; sie täuschen
den Tag, die Nacht, die Tiere und das Kind;
ihr Schweigen lügt, sie lügen mit Geräuschen
und mit den Dingen, welche willig sind.

Nichts von dem weiten wirklichen Geschehen,
das sich um dich, du Werdender, bewegt,
geschieht in ihnen. Deiner Winde Wehen
fällt in die Gassen, die es anders drehen,
ihr Rauschen wird im Hin- und Wiedergehen
verwirrt, gereizt und aufgeregt.

And during spring when only a few
have remained around my bed,
then I will shine by playing the harp
so sweetly as the northern April days
worried about each leaf—since they are late.

For my voice will have grown in two directions,
becoming scent, becoming cry:
one preparing the traveler from afar,
the other being mirror and angel and bliss
of my lonely days.

» » »

Give that both voices will be near
when again you dispense me into cities and fears.
With them I wish to be amidst the wrath of time,
preparing you a dwelling place from sound
in every place you want.

» » »

The teeming cities are a lie and deceive
the day, the night, the animals, and the child;
their silence lies, their noises too,
and all things that submit to them.

Nothing of significance or actual events
that circle around you, the becoming one,
happen there. The gusts of your wind
drop in the streets, which contort them
so their sounds through the steady pitter-patter
become confused, shrill, and nervous.

Sie kommen auch zu Beeten und Alleen—:

» » »

Denn Gärten sind,—von Königen gebaut,
die eine kleine Zeit sich drin vergnügten
mit jungen Frauen, welche Blumen fügten
zu ihres Lachens wunderlichen Laut.
Sie hielten diese müden Parke wach;
sie flüsterten wie Lüfte in den Büschen,
sie leuchteten in Pelzen und in Plüschen,
und ihre Morgenkleider Seidenrüschen
erklangen auf dem Kiesweg wie ein Bach.

Jezt gehen ihnen alle Gärten nach—
und fügen still und ohne Augenmerk
sich in des fremden Frühlings helle Gammen
und brennen langsam mit des Herbstes Flammen
auf ihrer Äste großem Rost zusammen,
der kunstvoll wie aus tausend Monogrammen
geschmiedet scheint zu schwarzem Gitterwerk.

Und durch die Gärten blendet der Palast
(wie blasser Himmel mit verwischtem Lichte),
in seiner Säle welke Bilderlast
versunken wie in innere Gesichte,
fremd jedem Feste, willig zum Verzichte
und schweigsam und geduldig wie ein Gast.

» » »

Dann sah ich auch Paläste, welche leben;
sie brüsten sich den schönen Vögeln gleich,

The winds even reach to the flower beds and alleys.

》 》 》

But gardens are true—built by kings,
who frolicked there for a little while
with some young women adding flowers
to their laughter's wonderful sound.
They kept these tired parks awake;
they whispered like breezes in bushes,
they alighted in furs and velvets,
and the silken ruffles of their morning dress
sounded like a creek on the graveled path.

Now all gardens follow them—
and infuse surreptitiously
themselves into the spring's coming
and slowly burn the autumn's flames
unto the great grate of their limbs,
a grate of thousands of monograms
cast artfully like wrought iron, dark.

And through the gardens peeks the palace
(like whitish sky with wiped-off light),
with its halls decked in ancient paintings
that hang immersed in themselves;
so willing to scale down, a stranger to each feast
and silent and patient as a guest.

》 》 》

Then I saw palaces that throb with life,
boasting and strutting like colorful birds

die eine schlechte Stimme von sich geben.
Viele sind reich und wollen sich erheben,—
aber die Reichen *sind* nicht reich.

Nicht wie die Herren deiner Hirtenvölker,
der klaren, grünen Ebenen Bewölker
wenn sie mit schummerigem Schafgewimmel
darüber zogen wie ein Morgenhimmel.
Und wenn sie lagerten und die Befehle
verklungen waren in der neuen Nacht,
dann wars, als sei jetzt eine andre Seele
in ihrem flachen Wanderland erwacht—:
die dunklen Höhenzüge der Kamele
umgaben es mit der Gebirge Pracht.

Und der Geruch der Rinderherden lag
dem Zuge nach bis in den zehnten Tag,
war warm und schwer und wich dem Wind nicht aus.
Und wie in einem hellen Hochzeitshaus
die ganze Nacht die reichen Weine rinnen:
so kam die Milch aus ihren Eselinnen.

Und nicht wie jene Scheichs der Wüstenstämme,
die nächtens auf verwelktem Teppich ruhten,
aber Rubinen ihren Lieblingsstuten
einsetzen ließen in die Silberkämme.

Und nicht wie jene Fürsten, die des Golds
nicht achteten, das keinen Duft erfand,
und deren stolzes Leben sich verband
mit Ambra, Mandelöl und Sandelholz.

and giving off a bad song.
Many are rich and want to rise—
but the rich are not rich at all.

Unlike your shepherds of sheep,
the dwellers of the greening plains
when they with their teeming and brimming herds
covered the plains like the morning sky.
And when they rested, with their commands
abated by the approaching night,
it was as if a soul awoke,
a different one, in the land they roamed—
and the camels' dark silhouettes
surrounded the land like hills.

And the aroma of cattle herds
lingered for another ten days,
warm and sweet and not heeding the wind.
And like in a lighted wedding house
the many wines run the entire night,
the milk ran from their donkeys' udders.

Unlike the sheiks of desert tribes
that slept at night on worn-out rugs,
but had rubies implanted in the gear
of their favorite mares.

Unlike the princes that threw about
their gold, which was never fragrant,
and whose proud living tied itself to
almond oil, sandalwood, amber.

Nicht wie des Ostens weißer Gossudar,
dem Reiche eines Gottes Recht erwiesen;
er aber lag mit abgehärmtem Haar,
die alte Stirne auf des Fußes Fliesen,
und weinte,—weil aus allen Paradiesen
nicht *eine* Stunde seine war.

Nicht wie die Ersten alter Handelshäfen,
die sorgten, wie sie ihre Wirklichkeit
mit Bildern ohnegleichen überträfen
und ihre Bilder wieder mit der Zeit;
und die in ihres goldnen Mantels Stadt
zusammgefaltet waren wie ein Blatt,
nur leise atmend mit den weißen Schläfen . . .

Das waren Reiche, die das Leben zwangen
unendlich weit zu sein und schwer und warm.
Aber der Reichen Tage sind vergangen,
und keiner wird sie dir zurückverlangen,
nur mach die Armen endlich wieder arm.

» » »

Sie sind es nicht. Sie sind nur die Nicht-Reichen,
die ohne Willen sind und ohne Welt;
gezeichnet mit der letzten Ängste Zeichen
und überall entblättert und entstellt.

Zu ihnen drängt sich aller Staub der Städte,
und aller Unrat hängt sich an sie an.
Sie sind verrufen wie ein Blatternbette,
wie Scherben fortgeworfen, wie Skelette,

Not like the white emperor of the East
who was fit for the kingdoms of a god;
but who lay outstretched with listless hair,
the old brow on the tile-covered floor,
and cried—because nowhere in paradise
even *one* hour was his.

Unlike the merchants of old trading ports,
who made sure to outdo reality
with their magnificent paintings,
and their paintings were outdone by events;
and those enfolded amidst the golden cloak
of the city folded up like a sheet, and breathed
barely with temples so white.

These were the rich who forced life to be
infinitely wide and heavy and warm.
But the days of the rich are long gone,
no one will ask you for them anymore;
only make the poor again poor.

» » »

The poor are not poor. They're only the nonrich,
who are without will and world;
marked by the imprints of ultimate fears,
they are disfigured all over and unfurled.

They attract the dust of the cities,
and every kind of garbage clings to them.
Disdained like sheets that are smallpox infested,
discarded like potsherds, like skeletons,

wie ein Kalender, dessen Jahr verrann,—
und doch: wenn deine Erde Nöte hätte:
sie reihte sie an eine Rosenkette
und trüge sie wie einen Talisman.

Denn sie sind reiner als die reinen Steine
und wie das blinde Tier, das erst beginnt,
und voller Einfalt und unendlich Deine
und wollen nichts und brauchen nur das *Eine:*

so arm sein dürfen, wie sie wirklich sind.

» » »

Denn Armut ist ein großer Glanz aus Innen . . .

» » »

Du bist der Arme, du der Mittellose,
du bist der Stein, der keine Stätte hat,
du bist der fortgeworfene Leprose,
der mit der Klapper umgeht vor der Stadt.

Denn dein ist nichts, so wenig wie des Windes,
und deine Blöße kaum bedeckt der Ruhm;
das Alltagskleidchen eines Waisenkindes
ist herrlicher und wie ein Eigentum.

Du bist so arm wie eines Keimes Kraft
in einem Mädchen, das es gern verbürge
und sich die Lenden preßt, daß sie erwürge
das erste Atmen ihrer Schwangerschaft.

like a calendar of last year—and still:
if your earth were in great need,
she would string the poor on a rosary
and carry them for a charm.

For they are purer than precious stones,
and like an animal just born,
and so naive and forever yours,
asking for nothing and needing just this:

being allowed to be this poor.

» » »

For poverty is a great gleam from within. . . .

» » »

You are the poor one, the deprived,
you are the stone without a bed,
you are the leprous outcast, banned
from town with rattle in hand.

For you own nothing, like the wind;
and glory is near all you have to wear;
the working dress of an orphan is more
luxurious, and at least owned.

You are as poor as the strength of a seed
in a girl, who would like to hide it
and pushes her loins so as to subdue
the first breath of her pregnant state.

Und du bist arm: so wie der Frühlingsregen,
der selig auf der Städte Dächer fällt,
und wie ein Wunsch, wenn Sträflinge ihn hegen
in einer Zelle, ewig ohne Welt.
Und wie die Kranken, die sich anders legen
und glücklich sind; wie Blumen in Geleisen
so traurig arm im irren Wind der Reisen;
und wie die Hand, in die man weint, so arm. . . .

Und was sind Vögel gegen dich, die frieren,
was ist ein Hund, der tagelang nicht fraß,
und *was* ist gegen dich das Sichverlieren,
das stille lange Traurigsein von Tieren,
die man als Eingefangene vergaß?

Und alle Armen in den Nachtasylen,
was sind sie gegen dich und deine Not?
Sie sind nur kleine Steine, keine Mühlen,
aber sie mahlen doch ein wenig Brot.

Du aber bist der tiefste Mittellose,
der Bettler mit verborgenem Gesicht;
du bist der Armut große Rose,
die ewige Metamorphose
des Goldes in das Sonnenlicht.

Du bist der leise Heimatlose,
der nichtmehr einging in die Welt:
zu groß und schwer zu jeglichem Bedarfe.
Du heulst im Sturm. Du bist wie eine Harfe,
an welcher jeder Spielende zerschellt.

You are so poor: like a sprinkling in spring,
which happily drops on the city's roofs,
and like a dream that prisoners have,
shut forever off from the world.
And like the sick, who are ill at ease
and are happy; like flowers in railroad tracks,
so sad and poor in mad travel wind; and
like a hand one weeps into, so poor. . . .

And what are freezing birds, compared to you;
what is a dog who for days went without food;
and what is one's being spent and lost;
and the quiet, long sadness of an animal
one has locked up and forgot.

And all the poor in the shelters,
what are they compared to you in your pain?
They are only small pebbles, not millstones;
yet even they can grind out some grain.

But you are the most destitute,
the beggar with the hidden face,
poverty's epitome,
the eternal metamorphosis
of gold exposed to sun.

You are the quiet one without a land,
not entering the world anymore:
too big and unwieldy for use.
You wail in the storm. You are like the harp
on which every player is crushed.

» » »

Du, der du weißt, und dessen weites Wissen
aus Armut ist und Armutsüberfluß:
Mach, daß die Armen nichtmehr fortgeschmissen
und eingetreten werden in Verdruß.
Die andern Menschen sind wie ausgerissen;
sie aber stehn wie eine Blumen-Art
aus Wurzeln auf und duften wie Melissen
und ihre Blätter sind gezackt und zart.

» » »

Betrachte sie und sieh, was ihnen gliche:
sie rühren sich wie in den Wind gestellt
und ruhen aus wie etwas, was man hält.
In ihren Augen ist das feierliche
Verdunkeltwerden lichter Wiesenstriche,
auf die ein rascher Sommerregen fällt.

» » »

Sie sind so still; fast gleichen sie den Dingen.
Und wenn man sich sie in die Stube lädt,
sind sie wie Freunde, die sich wiederbringen,
und gehn verloren unter dem Geringen
und dunkeln wie ein ruhiges Gerät.

Sie sind die Wächter bei verhängten Schätzen,
die sie bewahren, aber selbst nicht sahn,—
getragen von den Tiefen wie ein Kahn,
und wie das Leinen auf den Bleicheplätzen
so ausgebreitet und so aufgetan.

》 》 》

You, who are knowledge, and whose knowledge springs
from poverty and poverty's abundance:
Allow that the poor are no longer discarded
and crushed in despair underfoot.
All others are so uprooted;
but the poor grow from roots sublime,
like flowers, and smell like mint
and their leaves are jagged and fine.

》 》 》

Observe them and to what they compare:
they stir like suspended in midair
and rest as if being held up.
And in their eyes reigns the festive, dark
appearance of lighted leas,
drenched in a quick summer rain.

》 》 》

They are so quiet—almost resembling things.
And when one invites them over,
they are like friends who have returned;
they disappear among all that's small
and keep in back like a retired tool.

They are like guards of draped-off treasures
they keep safe, but never saw themselves—
carried by the depths like a boat,
and like the linen where it is bleached out—
so extended and vast and opened up.

» » »

Und sieh, wie ihrer Füße Leben geht:
wie das der Tiere, hundertfach verschlungen
mit jedem Wege; voll Erinnerungen
an Stein und Schnee und an die leichten, jungen
gekühlten Wiesen, über die es weht.

Sie haben Leid von jenem großen Leide,
aus dem der Mensch zu kleinem Kummer fiel;
des Grases Balsam und der Steine Schneide
ist ihnen Schicksal,—und sie lieben beide
und gehen wie auf deiner Augen Weide
und so wie Hände gehn im Saitenspiel.

» » »

Und ihre Hände sind wie die von Frauen,
und irgendeiner Mutterschaft gemäß;
so heiter wie die Vögel wenn sie bauen,—
im Fassen warm und ruhig im Vertrauen,
und anzufühlen wie ein Trinkgefäß.

» » »

Ihr Mund ist wie der Mund an einer Büste,
der nie erklang und atmete und küßte
und doch aus einem Leben das verging
das alles, weise eingeformt, empfing
und sich nun wölbt, als ob er alles wüßte—
und doch nur Gleichnis ist und Stein und Ding . . .

》 》 》

And look at the paths of their feet:
like those of animals, so convoluted
with every turn; and full of memories
of stone and snow and the cooled leas,
light and young, over which they go.

They have a share of this great pain
of which the human life is but a piece;
the balm of grass, the blade of stones
are both their lot—and both they love
and walk to your delight,
like hands that play the harp.

》 》 》

Their hands are like those of women,
as if those hands held motherhood;
as carefree as the birds when building—
when touching warm and calm in their trust,
and easily held like a cup.

》 》 》

Their mouth is like the mouth of a bust
that never spoke or breathed or kissed
and yet was of a life now gone,
receiving everything, ordering it well,
and now forming its lips as if it knew—
though it's only metaphor and thing and stone.

»»»

Und ihre Stimme kommt von ferneher
und ist vor Sonnenaufgang aufgebrochen,
und war in großen Wäldern, geht seit Wochen,
und hat im Schlaf mit Daniel gesprochen
und hat das Meer gesehn, und sagt vom Meer.

»»»

Und wenn sie schlafen, sind sie wie an alles
zurückgegeben was sie leise leiht,
und weit verteilt wie Brot in Hungersnöten
an Mitternächte und an Morgenröten,
und sind wie Regen voll des Niederfalles
in eines Dunkels junge Fruchtbarkeit.

Dann bleibt nicht *eine* Narbe ihres Namens
auf ihrem Leib zurück, der keimbereit
sich bettet wie der Samen jenes Samens,
aus dem du stammen wirst von Ewigkeit.

»»»

Und sieh: ihr Leib ist wie ein Bräutigam
und fließt im Liegen hin gleich einem Bache,
und lebt so schön wie eine schöne Sache,
so leidenschaftlich und so wundersam.
In seiner Schlankheit sammelt sich das Schwache,
das Bange, das aus vielen Frauen kam;
doch sein Geschlecht ist stark und wie ein Drache
und wartet schlafend in dem Tal der Scham.

» » »

And their voice comes from afar
as if it had left before sunset
and crossed great forests, had spoken
for weeks with Daniel in a dream—
and had seen the sea, and talks of it.

» » »

And when asleep, they are as if
returned to what did rent them out;
are offered like bread during famine
to midnight darkness and morning red,
and are like rain full of drizzling into
the young growth that waits in the dark.

Then there remains not even one scar
of their name upon their body, prepared to sprout
and bedded like the seed of that seed
from which you stem forevermore.

» » »

And look: their body is like a groom
and flows while reclining much like a brook,
and lives so fair just like a pleasant thing,
so passionate and so miraculous.
Amidst this body's slenderness collects the weak,
the worried, stemming from a woman's frame;
yet its makeup is strong and, like a dragon,
lies dormant in the valley of shame.

» » »

Denn sieh: sie werden leben und sich mehren
und nicht bezwungen werden von der Zeit,
und werden wachsen wie des Waldes Beeren
den Boden bergend unter Süßigkeit.

Denn selig sind, die niemals sich entfernten
und still im Regen standen ohne Dach;
zu ihnen werden kommen alle Ernten,
und ihre Frucht wird voll sein tausendfach.

Sie werden dauern über jedes Ende
und über Reiche, deren Sinn verrinnt,
und werden sich wie ausgeruhte Hände
erheben, wenn die Hände aller Stände
und aller Völker müde sind.

» » »

Nur nimm sie wieder aus der Städte Schuld,
wo ihnen alles Zorn ist und verworren
und wo sie in den Tagen aus Tumult
verdorren mit verwundeter Geduld.

Hat denn für sie die Erde keinen Raum?
Wen sucht der Wind? Wer trinkt des Baches Helle?
Ist in der Teiche tiefem Ufertraum
kein Spiegelbild mehr frei für Tür und Schwelle?
Sie brauchen ja nur eine kleine Stelle,
auf der sie alles haben wie ein Baum.

» » »

For see: they will live and multiply
unconquered by the battles of time;
they will grow like wild berries
and cover the ground with sweets.

For blessed are those that never stopped
standing calmly outside in the rain;
to them will come all harvests,
and their ripe fruit will be numerous.

They will outlast any end
and any kingdom whose meaning is gone;
they will rise like rested hands
when the hands of all other classes
and nations are worn.

» » »

Only take them away from the cities' sin—
the wrath and confusion they have to endure,
where during days of tumult they dry up
with patience injured.

Is there no room for the poor on the earth?
Who is the wind looking for?
And who drinks the light of the brook?
Is there no room in ponds for the sill and door's reflection?
They only need a small nook
for their necessities, like the trees.

Des Armen Haus ist wie ein Altarschrein.
Drin wandelt sich das Ewige zur Speise,
und wenn der Abend kommt, so kehrt es leise
zu sich zurück in einem weiten Kreise
und geht voll Nachklang langsam in sich ein.

Des Armen Haus ist wie ein Altarschrein.

Des Armen Haus ist wie des Kindes Hand.
Sie nimmt nicht, was Erwachsene verlangen;
nur einen Käfer mit verzierten Zangen,
den runden Stein, der durch den Bach gegangen,
den Sand, der rann, und Muscheln, welche klangen;
sie ist wie eine Waage aufgehangen
und sagt das allerleiseste Empfangen
langschwankend an mit ihrer Schalen Stand.

Des Armen Haus ist wie des Kindes Hand.

Und wie die Erde ist des Armen Haus:
Der Splitter eines künftigen Kristalles,
bald licht, bald dunkel in der Flucht des Falles;
arm wie die warme Armut eines Stalles,—
und doch sind Abende: da ist sie alles,
und alle Sterne gehen von ihr aus.

» » »

Die Städte aber wollen nur das Ihre
und reißen alles mit in ihren Lauf.

》》》

The house of the poor is like an altar.
In it the eternal transforms into food;
and at evening it quietly returns
in a wide circle and retreats
slowly and reverberates.

The house of the poor is like an altar.

The house of the poor is like a child's hand.
It will not even dare reach for what adults demand:
only a beetle with ornate tongs,
the stone rounded and smoothed by the creek,
the sand that ran, and shells that rang;
this hand is like a suspended scale
and indicates the smallest receiving
for a long time by the position of its pans.

The house of the poor is like a child's hand.

Like the earth is the house of the poor:
The splinter of a crystal yet to be,
soon bright, then dark in the flight of the fall;
poor like the warm simplicity of a barn—
and still the night comes; then the earth is the throne,
and the stars spread from her alone.

》》》

But the cities only crave selfishly
and carry everything away in their course.

Wie hohles Holz zerbrechen sie die Tiere
und brauchen viele Völker brennend auf.

Und ihre Menschen dienen in Kulturen
und fallen tief aus Gleichgewicht und Maß,
und nennen Fortschritt ihre Schneckenspuren
und fahren rascher, wo sie langsam fuhren,
und fühlen sich und funkeln wie die Huren
und lärmen lauter mit Metall und Glas.

Es ist, als ob ein Trug sie täglich äffte,
sie können gar nicht mehr sie selber sein;
das Geld wächst an, hat alle ihre Kräfte
und ist wie Ostwind groß, und sie sind klein
und ausgeholt und warten, daß der Wein
und alles Gift der Tier- und Menschensäfte
sie reize zu vergänglichem Geschäfte.

» » »

Und deine Armen leiden unter diesen
und sind von allem, was sie schauen, schwer
und glühen frierend wie in Fieberkrisen
und gehn, aus jeder Wohnung ausgewiesen,
wie fremde Tote in der Nacht umher;
und sind beladen mit dem ganzen Schmutze,
und wie in Sonne Faulendes bespien,—
von jedem Zufall, von der Dirnen Putze,
von Wagen und Laternen angeschrien.

Und gibt es einen Mund zu ihrem Schutze,
so mach ihn mündig und bewege ihn.

Like hollow wood they break apart the animals
and consume the nations by their flames.

And their inhabitants serve some particular culture
and lose their balance and their modesty,
and call their snail's paths progress,
and drive now faster where they once slowed down,
and sell themselves and dress like prostitutes,
and rattle louder yet their metal and glass.

Deception makes daily a fool of them;
they can no longer be themselves;
money's power grows, owns all their energies,
and is as potent as an easterly wind, while they are small
and hollowed and are waiting for the wine
and all poison of animal and human juices
to arouse them to a futile game.

» » »

And your poor are suffering under these
and are made heavy by all they see
and are freezing as with fever—aglow
and, expelled from every habitation, going
like foreign ghosts amidst the night;
and are so burdened by this dirt,
are like fungus spewed on in sunlight—
are yelled at by every happenstance,
by the whore's outfit, by vehicles, and lights.

And if there be a mouth for their protection,
let it be wise and move its lips.

O wo ist der, der aus Besitz und Zeit
zu seiner großen Armut so erstarkte,
daß er die Kleider abtat auf dem Markte
und bar einherging vor des Bischofs Kleid.

Der Innigste und Liebendste von allen,
der kam und lebte wie ein junges Jahr;
der braune Bruder deiner Nachtigallen,
in dem ein Wundern und ein Wohlgefallen
und ein Entzücken an der Erde war.

Denn er war keiner von den immer Müdern,
die freudeloser werden nach und nach,
mit kleinen Blumen wie mit kleinen Brüdern
ging er den Wiesenrand entlang und sprach.
Und sprach von sich und wie er sich verwende
so daß es allem eine Freude sei;
und seines hellen Herzens war kein Ende,
und kein Geringes ging daran vorbei.

Er kam aus Licht zu immer tieferm Lichte,
und seine Zelle stand in Heiterkeit.
Das Lächeln wuchs auf seinem Angesichte
und hatte seine Kindheit und Geschichte
und wurde reif wie eine Mädchenzeit.

Und wenn er sang, so kehrte selbst das Gestern
und das Vergessene zurück und kam;
und eine Stille wurde in den Nestern,
und nur die Herzen schrieen in den Schwestern,
die er berührte wie ein Bräutigam.

O where is the one who outgrew possessions and time
and grew strong and matured into poverty,
so that he took off his clothes in the market square
and walked naked before the authorities?

Where is this kindest and most loving of all,
who came and lived like the young year;
the brown brother of your nightingales,
in whom one finds amazement and mirth,
even rapture at the sight of this earth?

For he was none of those who grow
ever more tired and slowly lose their joy.
With little flowers like with little brothers
he walked along the meadow's rim and spoke.
He told of himself, how he employed
himself to become to everyone a joy;
and there was no end to his sunny heart,
and not even the small he ignored.

He traveled from light to ever brighter light,
and his cell stood amidst serenity.
The smile kept on growing on his face
and had its childhood and history
and became ripe as with puberty.

And when he sang, even the yesterday
and the long-forgotten returned;
and it became quiet in every room,
and only the sisters' hearts were stirred,
for he touched them like a groom.

Dann aber lösten seines Liedes Pollen
sich leise los aus seinem roten Mund
und trieben träumend zu den Liebevollen
und fielen in die offenen Corollen
und sanken langsam auf den Blütengrund.

Und sie empfingen ihn, den Makellosen,
in ihrem Leib, der ihre Seele war.
Und ihre Augen schlossen sich wie Rosen,
und voller Liebesnächte war ihr Haar.

Und ihn empfing das Große und Geringe.
Zu vielen Tieren kamen Cherubim
zu sagen, daß ihr Weibchen Früchte bringe,—
und waren wunderschöne Schmetterlinge:
denn ihn erkannten alle Dinge
und hatten Fruchtbarkeit aus ihm.

Und als er starb, so leicht wie ohne Namen,
da war er ausgeteilt: sein Samen rann
in Bächen, in den Bäumen sang sein Samen
und sah ihn ruhig aus den Blumen an.
Er lag und sang. Und als die Schwestern kamen,
da weinten sie um ihren lieben Mann.

» » »

O wo ist er, der Klare, hingeklungen?
Was fühlen ihn, den Jubelnden und Jungen,
die Armen, welche harren, nicht von fern?

Was steigt er nicht in ihre Dämmerungen—
der Armut großer Abendstern.

But then the pollen of his song
fell off his rose-red lips
and drifted dreamily to the lovingly kind
and dropped into the opened corollas
and slowly sank into their cups and minds.

And they received him, the unblemished one,
into their body, which was their soul.
And their eyes closed up like roses,
and full of passionate nights was their hair.

And both the great and the small received him.
And many animals were told by cherubim
that their mate was bearing fruit—
by angels that were beautiful butterflies:
and he was recognized by everything
for everything gave birth through him.

And when he died, so light and without name,
he was dispensed: his semen ran in creeks,
his semen sang in trees and saw
itself in the flower's cup.
It reposed and sang. And when the sisters came
they wept for the man they had loved.

» » »

Where is this sounding one, this clear one, gone?
Do not the poor who persevere
feel him, the joyous one and young?

Does he not climb into their dusks—
as poverty's great evening star?

Translator's Notes

3 *The clock has struck* The young Russian monk, living in a monastery, hears the clock strike, which rouses him to his activity of painting iconography.

3 *I live my life* The monk lives his life in expanding, ever-widening circles, which have God as their center.

5 *I have many brothers* Rilke refers here to the monks of Italy, who are hoarding in their monasteries the Renaissance masterpieces, such as those of the painter Titian, that depict God in radiance and magnificent splendor. In contrast to this depiction of God, the monk's God is humbly hidden, is active only underground, and is residing as in the life-bearing roots of a tree.

5 *We may not paint you* The icon artist relies on God's inspiration when painting, in addition to traditional technique. The nature of the icon is that it at once reveals and hides the deity or the saint depicted.

5 *I love the hours* The painter needs solitude, even a heightened sense of loneliness, to spur on his creativity. Throughout his life, Rilke lived by this tenet, seeking solitude and independence, even to the degree of avoiding intimate relationships if they threatened to become too involved. During the first year (1901) of his marriage to sculptor Clara Westhoff, for example, with his daughter already born, he had moved to Paris. When Clara followed him there, he insisted on separate apartments to preserve solitude for the sake of the creativity of both parties.

7 *You, neighbor God* The monk is concerned with God's well-being. He hopes that by his availability and openness to inspiration, the wall separating the monk and God might break down and the monk be guided to paint God's essence and true being. During this time God becomes known to the monk, though only for a short time.

9 *If only it were absolutely quiet here* Finding inspiration takes utter concentration and the blotting out of any distraction. Allowing inspiration to truly fill him would make the monk an instrument in the service of all creation.

9 *I live on the verge* Rilke wrote book 1 in 1899, the century's turn. There is a shift in address from God to a "you." The verses read, "One feels the wind as from a page, which God, and you and I, have written on. . . ."

The "you" could be either Lou Andreas-Salomé, to whom he entrusted and dedicated the entire manuscript, or anybody engaged in the activity of writing, or shaping history by an activity touching upon many people's lives.

11 *I conclude it from your Word* Wherever Rilke traveled, he carried a Bible with him. The poem alludes to the creation story and the first murder, committed by Cain on his brother Abel. God's goodness expressed in creation stands in sharp contrast not, as might be assumed, with the traditional Fall in the Garden of Eden and Adam and Eve's disobedience, but with the murder of Abel, which dispelled the voices that had "assembled to speak" to creation and the universe about God. The "loud scream" of Abel's has reduced the voices to but a stammer, so that God can be proclaimed only "in pieces."

11 *I do not exist* What follows is the pale boy Abel's dirge on the cessation of his life and a speculation on Cain's and humanity's plight. The murder of Abel is viewed as the beginning of original sin, which will result in inevitable death for all of humanity. Thus everybody becomes a victim of Cain's wrath. Abel finds comfort in the fact that he is now closer to God, the "night."

13 *You darkness whence I came* God is compared to darkness laden with possibility.

15 *I believe in everything that's never been said* The monk wants to express himself by means other than painting. Held captive by inspiration, he wants to give his talents free rein so as to "profess and proclaim" God as no one before him.

15 *I am much too alone in this world* Again the monk longs for utmost loneliness and a sense of humility, which will enable him to make the best use of his talents and time.

17 *I want to mirror* If the monk is not true to himself and doesn't have a clean conscience, he will, like a crooked mirror, reflect God inaccurately.

17 *You see I want much* The monk acknowledges his longing, or as Rilke called it in describing the artist, his *Sehnsucht,* to seek God and to find himself through service to and reliance on God.

19 *We build on you* Thus propelled, all those engaged in seeking and longing build reflections of God that are, in spite of their effort, incomplete. Works of art, the constructs of Rome, the church spires, the mile-long mosaics, can only scarcely reflect and compare with the grandeur of God. Only when the monk senses the concealed closeness

of God can he seek to add some marginal or final trim to his rendering of God.

21 *Someone desired you once* We may discard our traditional search for God, only to see God emerge and "wash forth" upon us in other ways.

21 *Whoever manages to reconcile* Finding God rests on the individual's ability to come to terms with life's blows. Doing so requires the same kind of loneliness God finds himself in all the time.

23 *Why should my hands* The monk describes here the person's activity of creating versus being created and being molded by God. The monk prefers the latter, where God imperceptibly moves in upon the monk's senses. God's moves take place in the background and can be noticed only when one has become quiet.

23 *I am, you timid one* The timid appearance of God is described; the monk eagerly and gently waits. The monk suggests that he would be willing to trade places with God so as to relieve God for a time of His responsibilities.

25 *My life is not made up* The monk argues for his proposal by addressing his biggest shortcoming, namely his busyness. He is as stolid as a tree, willing to be quiet, peaceful, and conciliatory.

25 *If I had grown up some other place* The monk regrets having to be engrossed in so much other toil that not enough time is left for proper worship and adoration, for more conversation and play and interchange with God. The monk admits to having had a chance of doing so once in a while. But the remembrance of this encounter has faded, like the laugh of old friends who live far away. As a result, God has become "small," like a young bird that, having fallen out of its nest, appears helpless and frightened.

29 *I find you in all these things* God can be found in all that is close and dear to us. In something as small as a seed, God is glorified as much as in any kind of greatness and excellence. The comparison with the seed is reminiscent of Jesus' parables of the seed and the parable of the mustard seed in Mark 4:26–32.

29 *I am hastily wasting away* Rilke has inserted here the voice of another person, a young fellow monk, who is struggling with his vows of chastity and poverty, so much so that he wants to die.

29 *See, God, there's another one* Now the first monk's voice is heard again, describing to God the other monk as a boy who is still torn between his childhood fancies, his religious upbringing, and his search for identity and service to God. It is likely that the monk can identify with the younger brother in the same way Rilke might identify with this monk. For Rilke too had been raised by a domineering, strictly Catholic mother, who boasted about having reared the child in rigorous religious practices. Rilke sees the younger brother only as one person in the course of Christianity who is called on to reflect God's glory, the "reflection of the sky above," until he again is replaced by "another face."

31 *I love you, you the gentlest law* The monk views God as law, but one that is gentle and beneficial for us. This law comes to us as a home-sickness, an inner *Sehnsucht* and longing to escape confusion, an increased self-restraint in our manner of speech, and a heightened sensitivity. Because this law is established, God can relax and even endure our per-petual offenses.

33 *Craftsmen we are* As builders of different degrees of skill, we seek to represent God, occasionally enlightened by someone coming into our life for a short time and giving us a better grasp and glimpse of God. In the process of our building on God, we may become inspired by God so that we are spurred on in our efforts and we at last glimpse Him in all his greatness.

35 *You are so great* In light of this vision of God's greatness and excellence, the monk comes to realize his own smallness and his wretched state. His only redeeming characteristic is that his longing for God is fierce. It is a longing that does not seek to lose itself in an "endless flight" of mystical trance or larger knowledge or frenzied activity dis-guised as service to God. Instead, it is a longing to come before God and experience his love, rather than condemnation.

35 *So many angels seek you* The monk does not find God in what is rep-resented by light, such as knowledge and "enlightenment," or the luminous and embellishing art of the Renaissance, for example. He thinks the angels have taken a wrong turn toward finding God. God elected to be found amidst the "light" only for a time, then went back home into the dark.

37 *These were the days of Michelangelo* The monk recognizes Michel-angelo's great genius because Michelangelo felt the "central theme of life," thus becoming the foremost representative of the Renaissance. Everything done during Michelangelo's epoch is gauged against his work. Yet Michelangelo became frustrated because, despite his great genius, God refused to be conquered in the same way as could God's cre-ation. In *Tagebücher aus der Frühzeit*, Rilke describes how Michelangelo's

genius was, by the same token, his downfall. If one had left Michelangelo to his own devices, Rilke writes, he would have chiseled out of this unshapely ball called Earth a slave, which later would have had to adorn his grave (97).

37 *The branch on God's tree spanning Italy* The monk feels that the branch called the Renaissance has already bloomed, but never bore fruit. In referring to the Renaissance artists as "spring artists," Rilke writes in his Florentine Diary that they never knew where they belonged, naively believing that "their white marble tombs were their homeland." Consequently, they were in no rush and moved toward building their dreams like churches (*Tagebücher aus der Frühzeit*, 68). Nevertheless, they managed to represent Jesus Christ well, so that in Italy he became the object of great worship and adoration.

39 *And then there was the shy and shaken maid* Besides Jesus Christ, the Renaissance artists also discovered as a subject for their art the Virgin Mary. The monk describes the development of various images of her, first as the "shy and shaken" Virgin, then as the "handmaiden" and servant of God, and finally as the "majestic and divine" mother of God.

41 *But then, as if the burden of too much fruit* The monk continues with the historic development of Mariology, which now depicts Mary in the role of bearer of great pain and suffering and thus, indirectly, as intercessor for the poor. Her pain includes rejection by and contempt from even the angels, who question whether she really had given birth to God's son.

41 *Thus one has painted her* The painter of the Virgin Rilke is referring to is probably Botticelli. About him, Rilke writes in his Florentine Diary that since "sentimentality requires weakness, a love for pain," no one exhibits it more than Botticelli. But it is not "a dull, unfocused sadness" but a sentiment of this fruitless spring (96).

43 *Through just one branch* The theme of the branch spanning Italy is picked up again. This time the branch does not resemble God, because it is a branch representing pain and loneliness. Only when people are lonely and "near tears" does God appear to them, though to each a different way. The monk resolves that through this state, the branch, and indirectly the root, "has borne its fruit" and encourages people to wake up and see. It is a seeing not of external color and form by the eye, but of the internal realization of God's nearness when one is lonely and in pain.

45 *I can't believe something small like death* In comparison to pain and loneliness, death seems small and even ridiculously insignificant. Still, we continue to be frightened and tricked by death as it appears to reach for us from within ourselves, "as if out of your coat."

47 *What will you do, God, when I'm dead?* The monk ponders God's need for people like him. The poem illustrates the interdependence between God and the person as colaborers, but carefully avoids giving the impression of arrogance or pride on the person's part. In these lines of potent imagery, Rilke beautifully expresses the sentiment of genuine caring for and responsibility toward God's well-being.

47 *You are the whispering sooty one* God is compared to the shade of a flickering oil lamp used in Orthodox services, the mysterious, whispering one, ever present though sublime and inconspicuous. By its subdued light, everything takes on a deeper sense. God is also compared to a syllable in song; not as the complete but the becoming God, who returns with the help of those who lend their voices in service and help in God's becoming whole. God is not flamboyantly attractive, but lowly, subtle, and simple.

49 *You stand perplexed* The monk addresses now the younger monk who is experiencing the torment of his senses and fleshly passions. In everything, temptation lurks, even in pious paintings. But then, at once, loneliness and reason set in, and the hands that did not give in to temptation hate their owner for preventing them from experiencing sensuous joy. Following this feat of the will, the young monk is able to hear again the rumors and perhaps even the voice of God.

51 *Then pray the way you were taught* The monk advises the younger one, presumably based on experience, how and what to pray in the aftermath of renounced earthly desires. The prayer contemplates the saints of the past, as well as future moments of temptation. Because of the prayer, the young monk is able to focus on "distant lands" which God will open up to him, beneath and past "the rolling hills."

53 *I have hymns that I keep to myself* The monk returns to addressing God again, confessing that the God he adores resides deep within him. At the same time, he sees how God views him, the monk, as a shepherd of others, who follow him and whom he seeks to lead.

53 *O God, how do I grasp your life* The monk is consumed by the desire to describe and depict God. He concludes that God experiences nothingness as pain; hence God sought healing by creating. At the same time that God experiences healing, this same healing touches upon creation. We know how healing has touched upon people in the past. Yet we, in the present, are foolish, for instead of admitting to the corruption of creation and its pain, we seek to conceal it by lying on it and about it. As a result, God's face grows more dim and distant.

55 *All who are apt to fold their hands* Still, there are those able to be honest with themselves, those who withdraw into solitude and prayer. And it is these who can "spell out" God and write him on a page. Ultimately, "only prayer exists," making God real, in fact, helping us realize that we are wedged into God like lobes in lava rock.

55 *The name we bear is like a light* We are individuals, which is symbolized by our names. Yet there comes a moment, as it does for the monk, when God confronts us as someone who demands that we share our individuality with Him. Over time, God wooed and wrestled with us so that we might give in and allow Him to become part of us. But then God is grieved over this victory, because He did not really know what He was bargaining for. Still, God faithfully embraces the creature who returns the love by caressing God's "old and grizzled beard."

57 *Your very first decree was: Light* Creation occurs in two stages. In the first stage, God creates light, hence time and history. In the second stage, God creates the human being and fear, resulting from the Fall and the first murder. As a consequence, the monk would rather not see the third stage of God's creative process. Instead, he desires God to become silently manifest in creation and in human behavior, so as to become our refuge from God's own wrath. This idea is symbolic of God's sending Jesus Christ, fully God and fully man, who becomes our refuge from God's wrath.

59 *You come and go* God visits creation quietly and gently. When God does so, the monk enjoys immersing himself in God's presence. Best of all, God's pulsating presence increases the monk's desire to work and be creative.

61 *You are the deepest, who looms tall* God is described in paradoxes, being both deep and tall; the diver and the tower's goal; the powerfully strong, who chooses self-restraint; the one to be rocked and caressed, who wields wrath on "people's backs."

61 *I know you are the rebuslike* The monk returns to being the painter of icons, who seeks to outline in careful detail what he is going to paint. But God thwarts his plans, so that the monk can paint only when inspired by God. As such, the painter becomes a medium through which God can "be always creating anew."

63 *Such is my daily labor* The activity of painting, of making art, is a form of worship. Art now becomes a proclamation of the Lord, a praise service, a resting in the arms of God. After this experience of worship, the monk rises and is left alone by both people and God. Yet he needs this loneliness to make him aware of his inner strength and great creative powers.

65 *How many of you, unbesieged cities* The monk's address switches from God to some "unbesieged cities," which might represent nations or individuals. He might be addressing all those who have never experienced being conquered by God, those who never learned to endure "the sadness, the hunger, the tears." God is waiting for them untiringly nearby. He will not seek to "threaten and promise" and beseech them. For God's speech is silent. Even so, it can topple the strongest walls people have built up between themselves and God.

65 *I am coming home from flying in circles* The monk admits to having lost himself once in high and lofty feelings of rapture. But he has come down now, has become more humble and more centered in his prayer. The monk compares this past spiritual ecstasy to a sense of having penetrated the sphere where the angels live. But he has concluded that these lofty heights are not the ground where God can be found. In fact, they are the nesting place of the angels' worst, namely Lucifer. He too had come to find out that God does not reside in lofty heights near the sun; that is why he "pleads for the dark." Yet this age, including its art forms, still seeks God high above, when God no longer dwells there and is hiding in the deep and dark instead.

69 *You're captured only through the deed* God is found not in tangible objects and outward form, but in deeds. Perceptions and one's senses can be misleading, for they do not display how God breaks into history and actively arrives, surrenders, and attacks those who try to run away from God. God is process and becomes known by process, not by static form. It matters little where God resides as long as one is able to "walk forever toward" the Lord.

71 *My life wears the same old dress and hair* The monk compares himself with the dead czars, who had power and kingdoms, while the monk has only "the empire of my mind" (the word *Gossudar* in the German original is a Russian word referring to a king or a king's empire).

The czars were flashy in their displays of piety, such as in their building frenzies, while the monk is reticent and quiet in his adoration of the Lord. In fact, the czars had gone so far as to quench every true expression and "gesture of trust" toward God. As a result, even churches and convents—edifices originally devoted to sacred worship and service—are makeshift gathering grounds of the semisaved, who are lulled into comfort by statues of saints and kings.

71 *And then God orders that I write* But God has ordered the monk to help the faithful wake up to this reality. The monk seeks to do so in three ways: By his writing, he can help people see that the cruelty of kings, or authorities of any kind, is necessary so people can recognize grace and love; by his painting, he can represent the reality of human sinfulness, squalor, and suffering; and by his building activity (perhaps in the decorative arts), he can establish historical markers that will, for generations to come, point people to God's activity in history.

73 *A thousand theologians dived* People of every profession and age have sought to identify and find God. Theologians have done so by analyzing the various names and natures ascribed to God; young women, especially those entering religious orders, have done so by taking God as their "spouse"; young men have done so by joining crusades. Poets have sought to identify God by exchanging with each other, and publishing, their impressions of God; musicians have done so by raising up and praising God's name; and even the past—in the form of history and one's memory examined—helps to shed light on God's glory.

75 *The poets scattered you about* The monk feels that he can represent God more authentically than the poets, and probably all others mentioned. After all, he has been searching for God long and hard, and he has collected the varied impressions into a single, representative collage. These impressions include the image of those who, as in Jesus' Sermon on the Mount, hungered and thirsted for God yet did not know where to find Him: the common laborer—the everyday person—who is numbed by work and uninterested in the spiritual world; the beggar with the smile that is prompted by the smallest kindness; and the sensitive child. The monk only wishes he could keep on working without interruptions, so that God can be made whole and the monk, by this work, become whole as well.

77 *There rarely is sun in Sobor* Recorded here are Rilke's reminiscences of his visit to the Uspensky Sobor, the Cathedral of the Assumption, which is one of the oldest edifices of the Kremlin and was, at the time, Russia's principal church. It was built in the fifteenth century by an Italian architect, Aristotle Fiorovanti, who had spent many years in Russia studying traditional architecture. The interior of the cathedral is austere and solemn, spacious, and illuminated only by two rows of narrow windows—hence it lacks sunlight. Rilke refers here to the church's gallery of rare icons, including probably the famous twelfth-century icon of the Virgin of Vladimir. Though the cathedral is topped by five gilt domes, Rilke is mainly interested in the interior's cupola that "ties together the entire dome." It is here that Rilke, in the voice of the monk, anticipates God's descent upon His throne.

79 *So I entered the church in piety* The monk enters the church and experiences God's presence as a "painful shock." For God seems to appear to these lowly, faithful, hardworking peasants who stop by at the church for brief periods of prayer and devotion. While witnessing how God reveals Himself to these peasants, the monk gains glimpses of God as a peasant.

81 *Like the guard who watches and waits* The monk's observation of the peasants leads to a contemplation of pastoral life. The monk wants to be a watchful guard in God's vast orchards. He longs to be an orchard or a fruit tree that never misses a round of bearing fruit for God.

81 *God talks quite audibly* Prior to birth, God has instilled a message in each person that encourages us to live life to the fullest, no matter the consequences, as long as we stay close to God without fear and are led by His hand.

83 *I lived with the oldest monks* The monk has studied the various art forms and the body of literature produced by monastic communities. He concludes that unlike his colleagues and predecessors, he prefers to be "modest and brief" in his art and his annals. For God does not distinguish between those who work in "cinnabar red and gold" and those who simply use ink from the tree's bark; between those who sow and plow deep in God the field and those who do not.

85 *You darkening ground* God is not only field but ground on which we build our walls against each other. He endures these walls, whether they be urban residences and fortifications, sacred buildings and monasteries, divisiveness and strife among the righteous, or the farmers' hard toil in eking out a living on his allotted parcel of land. Ultimately, in one sovereign move, God will shatter these walls and return everything to its original order. Until then, the monk wants to be a catalyst that redeems "things"—God's creation in general and nature in particular—and love them so they become worthy of being God's. This process of redemption the monk hopes to wield through the loving exercise of his art, which now is not only painting, but writing as well.

87 *I tend to wake up like a child* The monk's creative powers result from his childlike trust in God and an awareness of having to undergo perpetual change and growth "in quiet and behind closed doors" so as to become over and over again boy, child, and man.

87 *Do you realize that a few years ago* In reflecting on the quick stages from birth to adulthood, the monk wonders whether he is not rushing growth. Perhaps if he allowed God to change him gradually, he could be living in God's presence forever. People seek to precipitate their own growth by "seeking to escape" from God, who allows this sort of growth to happen. The most prominent evidence of such striving is people's frenzied activity of creating monuments of whatever kind unto themselves. All these "constructs" are a Tower-of-Babel type, for none has been "hewn by [God]."

89 *The light is making noises in your treetops* The apparent splendor and colorful wealth of things in the world detract from God's presence. Only the dark that smooths the color and blends forms can truly reveal God. The dark is kind and flattering even to what is "quaint and crude." It shows forth the same kindness that God has for the world, the same gentleness with which God envelops this globe. And like the dark, God is silent and quiet, for His power is already inherent in the world by the commands and laws He established from the beginning.

91 *You willing one, your mercy came* We are most likely to experience God's goodness and mercy during solitary prayers of repentance and confession. If we have such an experience, we will not boast about it. Instead, we will be concerned that God's name be guarded, that God's becoming real to us be shielded and kept safe from strangers and foes.

93 *Just one hour at the end of the day* It may be 11 P.M., all is dark, and the monk prepares his soul for encountering and conversing with God. The preparatory step for this encounter is an emptying of the mind. It is to become a vast plain of "heather and heath," dotted with ancient *Kurgane,* or burial mounds, representing the silence of the dead. Given the environment created by the soul is right, God will appear like an ancient and blind watchman, who goes from house to house to ring out the night

in song and melody. Even though God, the watchman, still wanders from house to house, He no longer has a voice: He has lost His message, that is, His songs, which have been taken from Him by time and people.

95 *And still I believe* But the monk believes these songs are not gone; rather, they are hiding somewhere deep within him. And while God, who has entered the monk's soul, is quietly looking for Himself, the monk supports God's knees, holds Him up, and manages to pour God's songs back into God. God has recovered His voice and has become God again.

THE BOOK OF PILGRIMAGE

97 *You, Pilgrim, are used to hurricanes* The monk views himself as pilgrim, as perpetual traveler, who has journeyed through valleys and up to mountaintops into such closeness to God that, in looking back, the experience seems like a summer retreat. During his retreat, the monk has experienced God being close and ever present. He feels that he has "reaped the fruit" of his pious efforts and wants to hold on to the experience. But he soon realizes that it cannot be done. Instead of reveling in the past, the monk needs to journey on and continue to be "like a tool for use" in God's hands.

99 *I am praying again, you blessed one* While in this "retreat mode," the monk had stopped praying. Now, in the aftermath of the spiritual high, he has difficulty doing so. Absorbed in a variety of experiences of depression, the monk feels himself "disjointed," particularly vulnerable and sensitive, and the target of ridicule and verbal abuse. The process of relearning how to pray is painful. Like a beggar in a back alley, he stammers at God for a handout, "petitioning to find again / a way to see your face!" The monk compares himself to an abandoned house, a city struck by the plague, and a stranger and adversary to his own mother. Nevertheless, he is unfaltering in his faith that God will reach for him again and the two of them become again a team.

101 *I'm still the same who often knelt* In many ways, the monk is the same person as before his spiritual renewal. He still seeks to faithfully serve the Lord in his station of life. And God is still the "wafting wave who hovers over all." Even the world is the same as before. The nations still seek to emerge from the chaos of the "vast sea" and progress toward an ordered universe. The angels still inhabit the peaceful quiet of the heavens. And God continues to be as silent as before.

Yet the spiritual renewal the monk experienced has also changed him. Like Job, he feels he has been a helpless target, an object, in God's hands. He is bold to question this passive status before God to which he had been relegated. He wonders why he does not receive more attention from God, especially when in pain and tears. And he begs God to listen to and answer his prayers and his "song" and restore mutual communion. After all, he is experiencing fear, hurt, and rejection, and God's presence would ease his pain.

Since God's absence has been all too real, the monk has to find reasons why God has withdrawn. "You probably don't know how those nights are," he speculates, nights when people feel overwhelmed by their guilt, and the spiritual void leaves them drained of all life. Rilke's imagery illustrates the state of loneliness and depression. In using an array of death symbolism, Rilke vividly describes the state of the person's estrangement from God.

The monk experiences this state of estrangement every day. But it is not so much on account of his own state, but that of others. He identifies with the lost, "who sought you in a fruitless walk," who "trip in the dark" with their prayer and their cries. It is on their behalf that he suffers and for whom he seeks to intercede by calling on God with humility.

107 *You, eternal one, did show yourself to me* This poem is a rather unorthodox description of the relationship between the believer and God. Rilke effectively develops and argues the view that the believer is like an old, protective father, while God is the young, adventurous, and energetic son.

109 *My prayers are to you no blasphemy* In this relationship, the believer/father realizes his status as the loving and caring relative of God. God is not a father, as orthodoxy presumes and as is stated in the first line of the Lord's Prayer. For a father is someone left behind, abandoned, ignored, or not to be taken seriously, especially as he grows old.

111 *And his meticulous ways are a nightmare to us* In old age, a father "grates . . . on our nerves." We "listen to barely half of his words," and the chasm between us deepens with every passing year. God is none of that, which makes it impossible, even blasphemous, that we should call him a father. God is a son, the only and much-loved child of ours, and we have been charged with God's growth and development.

111 *Extinguish my sight, and I can still see you* A father, or mother, can instinctively sense the child's whereabouts. A parent can relate to the child without a pedagogical instruction manual and can communicate without words. He or she can display caring for and a deep love of the child even under prohibitive conditions and in the absence of traditional means, such as adequate financial resources and time.

Rilke's lifelong friend and former lover Lou Andreas-Salomé claims that this poem was originally written for and dedicated to her. Though it may have romantic nuances, it more adequately illustrates a parent's love for a child.

113 *And my soul is like a woman to you* The poem is an allegory that compares the soul to the Old Testament character Ruth. The soul that is immersed in love for God is like the "band" that ties Ruth to Naomi, her mother-in-law. When Ruth says to Naomi, "Where you go, I will go; where you lodge, I will lodge" (Ruth 1:16 NRSV), she expresses a loving care and concern for her mother-in-law and, in a larger sense, for her neighbor. Thus, the soul is concerned with the well-being of one's neighbor. But the soul is also, and more important, the companion of Boaz, who represents God. By day, the soul shows love for God in service and labor. By night, as after the cleansing bath of confession and repentance, the soul visits God as her next of kin and draws close in worship and adoration.

113 *You are the heir* God as son has inherited our souls and will continue to "rise and grow" on account of them.

113 *And you inherit what grew* God inherits not only our souls but everything else too, such as the wonders of nature and those built by human hands. The decorative palace gardens of the past, the dew that has long since evaporated, the summers, the springs, the autumns, and the winters—all these are God's, as much as the rich imperial cities of both Italy and Russia, with their impressive historic sites.

Rilke visited all the cities and sites mentioned in this poem. In Italy, he had seen Florence, Pisa's cathedral, Venice, and Rome. In Russia, he had seen and heard the bells of Moscow, entered the underground monastery, the *lavra* (a word used by the Orthodox church to designate the largest and most important monasteries) at Kiev. This is the first reference to Kiev's Pechersk monastery with its "darkened tunnel's maze," which will be elaborated on later in the book.

All efforts in the arts, both literary and visual, are intended to be eternalizing pointers toward God. In fact, Leonardo da Vinci's Mona Lisa at the Louvre in Paris would suffice to represent a woman's beauty for all eternity. In a sense, then, artists resemble God in that they, like God, desire to create that which has eternal value.

But even lovers are collectors and distributors of eternal goods. As "poets for the shorter run," they dispense to their lovers a transforming joy and an agonizing pain by their passion and charm. And though they die, their stories may live on in their offspring and be recalled as ever-repeating epics of romantic tragedy and delight.

Every form of abundance, then, be it nature, artistry, or personal relationships, will add to God's inheritance and will eventually enrich and benefit God.

117 *I am one of your lowliest* The monk views himself as being closer to nature than to people. For people are not really alive. They are "accidents, pieces with voice," and detached from God's intended purpose for their lives. Even children, who are closest to their original design, learn early on to wear masks and to model adult, thus unauthentic, behavior. Ultimately, people lock themselves into behavioral patterns that render them spiritually inert and inaccessible to their neighbor and even to God.

119 *And yet, though everybody seeks to get away* Despite people's alienation from self, others, and God, life goes on and continues to pulsate in the world. The monk wonders who or what the bearer of life is. It might be creation with its winds, trees and flowers, and animals. But it might as well reside with God alone.

121 *You are the Ancient One* God is viewed as a strange old blacksmith, who is a master at His trade and always at work, even when everyone else is asleep. Because of His strange behavior, God is the talk of the town.

123 *Some rumors run suspecting you* God patiently endures the rumors that people are circulating. Some people believe in God's existence, others deny it, and still others ask for tangible proof. God could demonstrate His existence with mighty and miraculous acts. But He will not respond to their pagan demands. Neither will God force people to love Him, or argue them into the ground with clever strategy, or provide the skeptic with answers. Instead, God is concerned with those who keep quietly working at the task set before them.

125 *All who seek you put you to the test* Believers have sought to control God by tests and irrational demands. But the monk is not interested in that. His only wish is that God remain true to the laws established many generations ago.

125 *If something fell off my windowsill* One example of these long-established laws is the law of gravity, which takes effect even on "the smallest thing." God's law guards "[e]very single thing . . . as by kind wings ready for flight." In contrast to the rest of creation, humans have run counter to these laws God has ordained. "Instead of fitting into generous tracks / more willingly," we tend to violate nature, separate ourselves from the familiar in search of the new, and end up "utterly alone." We need to resist this willful independence and begin emulating the nature of things and their behavior. Gravity teaches us the direction we need to take—down on our knees in surrender before God. We are not alone in this posture. Even the angels are—contrary to mythical thought—not hovering above like nimble birds but are perched like penguins on the ground and listening to a God who is not high above but down below.

127 *You intend for us to be humble* The law of gravity teaches us humility. We bow before God, and along with God, in quiet moments of introspection. We join the common people, such as peasants, in their grief over a child's death. We pray with the praying and hurt with the hurting. And it is then that God becomes so real and tangible to us that even both neighbor and clock are viewed as interruptions. We have been sensitized to God's presence. As a result, God seems to be everywhere and we journey on as if on a cruise, or pilgrimage of sorts, where we lay anchor in small harbors and visit hamlets that tend to resemble each other. The impressions conveyed by our senses tend to repeat themselves and are unified by our focus on God. Even though we may find ourselves on unfamiliar terrain at times, we will be guided along the path as by a small horse-drawn carriage.

The poem reflects Rilke's trip up the Volga, as related in his letter of July 31, 1900, from Petersburg. On this journey, Rilke and Lou had traveled by ship as well as by small boat, and at one point had taken a small horse-drawn carriage, or troika, to explore the town.

131 *In this particular place the very last house* Journeying to the hamlet of one's utmost loneliness is dangerous. It affords us a view into both worlds, the one with and the other without God. One will never be able to stop on this pilgrimage and rest for good, for the path we travel does not lead up to a specific house, but instead goes alongside it.

131 *Sometimes, at the dinner table, a man might get up* This poem illustrates the restlessness of this pilgrimage. One person might get up and follow God's call toward a church in the East, while another one prefers the familiar surroundings of his home and hearth. The poem is reminiscent of Jesus' remark to the disciples not to look back but to follow Him, for "no one who puts a hand to the plow and looks back is fit for the kingdom of God" (Luke 9:62 NRSV). While the one leaving will invite conflict with his children—perhaps to the point of being "declared dead" or insane—the other will have to bear being abandoned by his children eventually and hence to finding the comfort of his home destroyed. Rilke seems to intimate what he considered his own lifelong tenet as a poet and family man: It is better to follow God's call into strange lands than to bask in the short-lived comfort of compromise.

133 *Folly is a sentinel* This poem is rather obscure. It probably refers to an incident reported by Lou Andreas-Salomé in her "Russian Diary." She and Rilke were staying in the small Russian town of Novinki, where the "sentinel was walking around with a tinkling triangle, on which three small bells charmingly intertwined their sounds." In the poem, folly is personified as a roaming sentinel, who walks the town's streets at night. The use of folly as a person also appears in the Old Testament Book of Proverbs, chapter 9, where folly is despised as surreptitiously inflicting harm upon the person, while wisdom is extolled. To Rilke, wisdom is of no concern. Instead, he depicts folly as a virtuous persona, who guards people's lives, and in whose company children are especially comfortable.

133 *Have you heard of those saints, Lord* Rilke refers here to the Pechersk Lavra, the underground monastery in Kiev, especially the religious order that founded it five hundred years earlier. Apparently, each monk lived in his solitary cell underground in accordance with the vows of silence, chastity, poverty, and fasting. Only on rare occasion would they assemble in the meeting hall and reflect on their common vision. The monks are portrayed as spiritually dead and emotionally crippled. Their austere way of life did not contribute to a deepened spiritual union with God.

Though their embalmed bodies lie preserved on display for tourists, they are not celebrated as heroes but as sad examples of an eccentric and lopsided spirituality. What is worse, they have not been released into a final stage of rest, but continue to exist on display in their half-dead state. Rilke addresses the tragedy of dying "only halfway" in the third book.

137 *You are the future, bright morning red* Only God transcends time and time's beginning and end. As St. Augustine holds, God lives

outside of time, is not subject to it, and thus commands it. Our human effort is to halt time, to replay it, or to advance it. God, on the other hand, simply is, living as "metamorphosis" amidst all things as their hidden essence.

139 *You are the shrine for stigmata* God is a sanctuary, a place of refuge for the stigmatized, the pained, the pierced. God lives in their midst, as well as in the many churches that are part of the Pechersk community and its surroundings. The impressive architecture of the settlement, the monastery's courtyard, and the great gate are testimony to God's presence. The quiet of the community is symbolized in an aestheticized depiction of the nuns' living quarters and an adjacent cemetery. The cemetery's tombstones represent the world of unbridled passion and deceit. They stand in stark contrast with the pious community as reminders of a period that has been superseded by the clandestine arrival and incipient rule of God.

141 *The kings of the world are old* The kings of the world do not have heirs who are strong or principled enough to carry on their parents' reign. This implies that a new reign, namely, a form of theocracy, is in the process of being established. The arrival of this new reign will be sped up because the source of power, namely, money and precious metal, is taking matters into its own hands and will return for good "from the factories and cash registers" to where it was wrested from.

143 *Everything will be magnificent again* When this reign, this new heaven and earth, arrives, creation and people will return to their intended state: The countryside will be unspoiled, the waters clear, the people clearly distinct against the virgin landscape as a herding and farming community. And churches will no longer be necessary as the former sanctuaries of a God that had been trivialized and belittled. People will trust each other and live in community. Death will no longer be euphemized but taken seriously. And so, instead of wasting time on trivialities, people will seek to refine their talents in service to creation and God.

143 *Even you, God, will be big* Even God will seem bigger. The previous burden wrought by human hands has been lifted, so God can readily roam and be easily felt. People, now content with less, will know what is good and love God as a matter of course. Collective prayer will have become unnecessary, for the believer will be naturally at home in a variety of worship practices and spiritual disciplines.

145 *There will never be apathy in the homes* Under this divine rule, apathy will be nonexistent. Too much is happening to become bored, either because people are dying or someone is being born into responding to God's call. The streets will be full of people journeying, as on a pilgrimage, toward God. This description goes back to an incident recorded in Lou's diary: While they were in Kiev, a million pilgrims were there to celebrate Pentecost.

147 *And that's how I want to journey to you* The poet returns to the initial "I," the Russian monk, who dreams about making a pilgrimage and living on charity. He sees himself being counseled by the elders of the pilgrims' throng as to where to go and then passing those who walk slower or have stopped for rest or water. With all these pilgrims, the monk feels a strangely intimate and pleasant bond.

147 *O God, I want to be many pilgrims at once* The monk wants to show his devotion to God by being more than just one person. For it is hard to serve and witness to God singularly; it is easier to be in a group of like-minded believers. Since he is only one person, the monk tends to become discouraged when ridiculed for his faith. Yet, by the same token, being in the minority and surrounded by nonbelievers lets him remain more anonymous in his religious activity and convictions.

149 *By day you are but secondhand sound* Appearances cover up the essence of God, for God's being is made known and experienced only in the stillness of the dark.

149 *It's morning on the pilgrimage* The voice changes back from the monk's to that of Rilke, who describes the large crowd of pilgrims and their children whom he saw in Russia rising from their sleep in the morning and washing at a fountain. Among them he finds people from all social strata, the troubled, the outcast, and the well-to-do. Aware of the meaninglessness of their life, they have become wise, "have been through much," and have grown increasingly dissatisfied with life as they know it. Now that they have embarked on a pilgrimage to God, they are the "slowly unfolding."

The second part of the poem deals with a sick monk who has an epileptic seizure. This incident, which occurred at the Pechersk monastery, is also reported in Lou's diary and must have left a deep impression on Rilke for him to refer to it as extensively as he does. The believer in the form of the epileptic monk appears as trying hard to gain God's attention. The monk goes through many extravagant motions of service and supplication, but God will barely bat an eye. Only when the monk tears off his robe and kneels in naked surrender does God respond and draw the man to Him.

157 *The red barberries are about to ripen* The poem breaks off the Kiev memory and picks up again the theme of the summer's retreat, which has come to an end. Whoever has not been enriched by the summer's fullness, by the experience of God's closeness at one point, will never find God. The person who denies the reality of God in the midst of great beauty and abundance is calloused and blind. Wrapped up in cynicism and denial, the person will then perceive God as a burden or heavy weight.

159 *Don't worry, God* The monk now addresses the possessiveness of human nature and tries to explain it to his God. A person in denial of God's creative abundance will seek to substitute the void with possessions and possessive pronouns. The human soul seeks to boast, elevating itself by citing famous acquaintances and calling one's own the dwelling, the past, the family, and the pet. This categorizing of possessions as mine and thine is done to make sense of, and bring order to, a confusing world. But certainty, Rilke says, "is only reserved for the wise, / those longing for eyes." There is wisdom in acknowledging our role as observant stewards, rather than boastful domesticators and lords, of creation. Yet even the faithful, "the one who loves [God] and can make out [His] face in the dark," calls God "my God." It will be of no consequence to God, for God cannot be domesticated, manipulated, or constrained.

161 *In long nights I dig for you, you gold* The last poem of book 2, "The Book of Pilgrimage," forms a transition to book 3, "The Book of Poverty and Death." The pilgrimage leads from digging in the ground for the "gold" of God to a hidden, abandoned, and overgrown path "no one has walked" in a long time. It is a search that makes all previous luxury experienced look like poverty in light of the true treasure to be sought and found. It is reminiscent of Jesus' parable of the hidden treasure, where the kingdom of heaven is compared to treasure hidden in a field and found by a man who in turn sells all he has and buys the field that holds the treasure (Matthew 13:44).

The poem concludes with a stunning image that symbolizes the believer's or the pilgrim's two postures before God. First, the believer has exerted great effort in digging for God, even to the point of tearing up the skin on his hands. But then the believer raises both hands heavenward without effort and exertion and is able to "absorb" the "fine particles" into which God has scattered as the soothing and sustaining "spring rains" and rays of hope they are.

THE BOOK OF POVERTY AND DEATH

165 *Like a piece of solitary ore* The poem appears to refer to the Pechersk Lavra's founding monks, who in digging caves were "crawling through mountainous veins." However, it is more likely that it alludes to Rilke's travel by train from Paris to Viareggio, Italy, where for long stretches the train tunneled through the Alps. The poem expresses a state of claustrophobia, secludedness, and depression, which corresponds with Rilke's own state of financial problems, ill health, and anxiety at the time of writing. The poet asks God to become "heavy and break through," so a reciprocal exchange can take place whereby each influences the other.

165 *You mountain who remained as the highlands formed* God is compared to a nameless and enormous mountain, which towers over creation, and is also its source. Though locked into and enclosed by this mountain, the monk still seeks to be of some use and of good service. The monk thinks it unjustified to surmise that God has locked him in, for the monk might be subconsciously interpreting his dislike of the large cities as God's confining activity. The large cities are representative of Paris, where Rilke had moved two years earlier. He complains to God about these cities' "erratic ways," though is willing to refrain from doing so and bear his lot humbly, though under great discomfort.

167 *Make me the guardian of your estate* The monk pleads with God to allow him to escape city life. He knows he would be of much better use in the country, would be God's faithful steward and guardian of His estate there, and blindly "keep near the faithful."

169 *For Lord, the major big cities are* This poem is a shockingly realistic description of the degenerative and spiritually repressive life in the city. People are estranged from nature, herded together in crowded basement flats lined by window wells that rest in the dark. Even the loveliness of youth and beauty, as in children and women, is drenched in sadness and subdued by quenched hopes.

171 *People live there white blossomed and pale* People in this urban landscape never grow into what they were destined to become, being alienated from self, with once tender smiles distorted into ugly faces. They have become unwitting work machines and victims of greed and capitalism. In their desolate state, they either seek escape in sickness or by trusting in modern medicine. They are spiritually dead already, but the physical death leaves them waiting and "hangs in them" like a sour green piece of fruit slow to ripen.

173 *O Lord, grant death to each in one's own way* The prayer of the monk is twofold: first, that God allow each person an individual and dignified death, not one that is mass administered in the hospital's death wards, and second, that God allow a person a life that has witnessed emotional width and depth, and hence stands in contrast to death, instead of agonizingly foreshadowing and preempting it.

173 *For we are only hull and leaf* We all carry the seed of death, the potential "fruit," within us and much of our frenzied effort and activity is prompted by the inevitability of this fruit's ripening. Girls and boys, mothers, artists, and architects all long and spin and turn and shape because death looms in the background. In fact, much of our emotional and intellectual activity is a product of our being aware of this fruit, which is so painfully slow in maturing.

173 *Lord, we are poorer than beasts* The animals at least can bring the fruit of death to maturity. Because they live fully, they are able to die fully, while "we can only die halfway." We have no control over birthing our own death, but instead are trapped in a lingering semidead state. Because we have been "whoring with eternity," have been flirting and hobnobbing with the eternal God and the Spirit that gives life, instead of fully surrendering to the divine forces, we bring forth by miscarriage a death that is not fully developed but resembles a "crippled, miserable embryo."

175 *Raise up one, Lord, who is glorious and great* The poem asks God to raise up a savior figure, who will bring death to us and on our behalf. This person will have experienced the heights and depths of true human living: a home in close proximity to God, the full experience of his own sexuality, a heightened power of sensuous perception, unadulterated and healthful living, and the recollection, grasping, and reliving of his childhood dreams and aspirations.

179 *But let the final round happen to us* Having raised this savior figure and this model of truthful, in-depth living, God is asked to appear "at the height of your might" and allow us to give birth at last to death in "a motherhood that is true." The poem plays on the doctrine of the virgin birth, whereby the Virgin Mary bore Jesus, the Son of God. The poet asks God not to grant another birthing of God, but instead to allow for a birthing of death. God has already been born unto the world and into the believer's heart. Now it is time that the believer learns to live this abundant life in God, so that a healthy and complete death can develop and mature as a result.

179 *I want to praise him* The language is reminiscent of the Old Testament and Israel's expectation of the Messiah. The monk sees himself dancing around the ark, as King David did, and being a prophet and evangelist of the new messianic pact or covenant. In his office of being God's mouthpiece, the monk wishes to be both scent and cry—both gentle introspective voice and warning siren.

181 *Give that both voices will be near* Since God is sending him back to the city, the monk asks to be equipped with both voices, the complete set, that is, so as to build God a dwelling place in whatever place the monk happens to be.

181 *The teeming cities are a lie and deceive* Again, the monk loses himself in an outburst against the big cities' deceitful appearance. Neither their silence nor their noises reflect reality. Worse yet, no significant happenings associated with or surrounding God take place there. Even the sound of wind, which God is sending, is contorted by the city's streets with their steady pitter-patter of feet.

183 *But gardens are true—built by kings* Still, the big cities offer certain oases of truth, namely gardens and parks. Many of them were built by kings to please their young women, who in turn filled them with life and laughter. All other, later gardens follow their example and represent by their seasonal changes a piece of God's reality in the city. Through these gardens is also visible from afar the royal palace that, with its ancient paintings, appears like a guest in its own environment and a stranger from another era.

183 *Then I saw palaces that throb with life* While some palaces are simply decorative bywork amidst their gardens and parks, there are others that are still filled with lively "boasting and strutting," possibly as seats of government. But despite their colorful and flamboyant appearance, they and their inhabitants and affiliates are not really rich. They are found wanting when compared to certain groups of people, such as shepherds and herders, chiefs of desert tribes who sleep on worn-out rugs, princes who knew how to live a refined—not just a pompous—lifestyle. The "white emperor of the East" may be a reference to Ivan IV, because the figure of an old man doing penance resembles that portrayed in Aleksei Tolstoy's *Death of Ivan the Terrible*, as well as a poem of Rilke's in *Die Zaren* (*The Czars*), where Ivan had murdered his son. The czar is rich not because he is ruler over a vast land, but because he does penance in atonement for his sins. The merchants of old trading ports are rich because they were wise enough to use their power to benefit the city's cultural life and history, instead of using it for merely personal gain. Though all these cited were truly rich, Rilke says these days are gone. Now it is the era of the poor, where the poor are allowed to be just that—poor.

187 *The poor are not poor. They're only the nonrich* The poem is a hymn in praise of the poor. Though they are "disfigured" and "unfurled," stained by the city's dust and garbage, and disdained, they are the earth's prayer beads, her rosary, and her good-luck charm. And since they are "purer than precious stones" and forever God's because of their innocence and naïveté, God should allow them "to be this poor."

189 *For poverty is a great gleam from within* For someone lacking worldly possessions, all attention is focused on the interior life. Consequently, the soul of the poor is the only thing remaining that is capable of shining, which it does.

189 *You are the poor one, the deprived* The poem compares God to the poor, since both have many things in common. Like the poor, God does not have a place of rest, a homeland or place of asylum, a protective outer garment, or a powerful appearance. Instead, God is like a stone, a leper, someone naked, or someone small and feeble like a seed. Among other images, God appears as the small shower in spring, the inmate's dream, the flower between the railroad tracks.

Even animals that are freezing, starving, or abandoned have it better than God. So do the homeless in shelters, for they can still set something in motion, while God is not only a beggar but a beggar who is hidden. God no longer has a platform or dwelling place in the world because the world considers God as "too big and unwieldly for use," so that only His wailing is heard in the storm.

193 *You, who are knowledge* The poem is a prayer on behalf of the poor to the one who, like them, draws knowledge from being poor. God is asked to grant justice to the poor, because they grow like God silently and underground in their roots, as does God when described as a tree in book 1.

193 *Observe them and to what they compare* This poem is an introduction to a litany of characteristics of the poor, illustrated in the eight poems that follow.

193 *They are so quiet—almost resembling things* The poor are unassuming and keep themselves in the background. They are uncomplicated and unaware of the deep riches they have to offer.

195 *And look at the paths of their feet* The direction of the life of the poor appears to be accidental, like that of animals, yet they consciously participate in life and its pain.

195 *Their hands are like those of women* The poor are caring, carefree, and approachable.

195 *Their mouth is like the mouth of a bust* The poor have experienced life's ups and downs and have cultivated a quiet receptivity.

197 *And their voice comes from afar* Because of the extremes they experience, the voice of the poor is steady and calm.

197 *And when asleep* The poor reflect the original state of innocence, which nurtures the earth.

197 *And look: their body is like a groom* The poor are aware of their own sensuousness and their bodies' natural beauty.

199 *For see: they will live and multiply* Because of all these abovementioned attributes, the poor will eventually come to reign in a kingdom without end. The language is reminiscent of the Beatitudes in the Sermon on the Mount (Matthew 5:3) and the Beatitudes in Luke, where Jesus says: "Blessed are you who are poor, for yours is the kingdom of God" (Luke 6:20 NRSV).

199 *Only take them away from the cities' sin* The major obstacle to the poor's inheriting this quiet and simple rule is the squalor of their urban surroundings, which taxes their patience.

201 *The house of the poor is like an altar* The house of the poor is not the city, but their heart and attitude. Rilke compares their interior to an altar where God resides, to a child's hand that receives even and especially small things with utter gratitude, to the earth that holds bright crystals and whose womb contains the essence of life.

201 *But the cities only crave selfishly* Urban development in the industrialized age contaminates people and destroys animal life, with greed in the guise of progress as the driving force.

203 *And your poor are suffering under these* The poor are the victims of greed and await deliverance by someone in authority issuing a word of hope or a wise decree.

205 *O where is the one who outgrew possessions and time* The poem alludes to St. Francis of Assisi, who, by his life and the rule of the Franciscan order he founded, exemplifies this word of hope. Following a conversion experience, Francis renounced his life of pleasure and luxury and was giving away his wealth. On one occasion, he took cloth goods from his father's business and sold them so as to help restore a painting at the church at St. Damian. As a result, his father brought him to trial in the market square before the authorities and the local bishop, who ruled that the son would forfeit his inheritance. In response to the verdict, Francis took off his clothes and returned them to his father, saying that from now on his only father would be his Father in heaven. The "brown brother" indicates the color of the Franciscan habit. The reference to nightingales and songs is an allusion to St. Francis's love of animals, particularly birds. The "sisters" refers to the order founded by St. Clare, who received her habit at the hands of St. Francis, and whose order, like that of the Franciscans, had the vow of poverty as its guiding tenet. Rilke seems to be subtly alternating between references to Orpheus and St. Francis, since both were known for their song and their love of animals, though the person and message of St. Francis remain prominent.

207 *Where is this sounding one, this clear one, gone?* The book ends by celebrating St. Francis as "poverty's great evening star." His song and example will live on and continue to promise hope to the poor and to all those who have exchanged worldly riches for the sake of a devout service to God.

About the Author

Rainer Maria Rilke (1875–1926) is the author of *Duino Elegies, The Sonnets to Orpheus,* and the novel *The Notebooks of Malte Laurids Brigge.* Bilingual editions of Rilke's *Duino Elegies* and *New Poems* are published by Northwestern University Press.